Welcome!

Hey there, beautiful!

Welcome to the first day of the rest of your life! You are about to embark on a beautiful journey of self-awareness to gain the momentum that you desire for your life. You are a powerful human and there is only one of you in the world. That is so cool! You have dreams, goals, and desires.

So, are you going to close your eyes in life or wing it and hope for the best? Or are you going to live your life with intentions, purpose, and passion? When we step into our power with clarity and confidence, amazing things happen!! I am inviting you to set some goals and intentions for the next twelve months of your life. HUGE goals! Yes, the ones you are scared about and the ones you have never told anyone. It is time! You get one life. It is not about perfection, getting everything right or chasing an invisible ideal. Instead, it is about living a fulfilling life with purpose — every single day. When we are Krystal Clear in the direction and know that we are in deep alignment with our goals, we figure out ways to show up as the amazing main character in our life!

In this planner, you will develop tools to backward plan, take necessary action, reflect, and celebrate life in full color! Action and momentum breed results and confidence--and we are better able to embrace the daily chaos of our life, work, family, and relationships. Life is tough stuff. But it also gets to be filled with fun, passion, and purpose. Yes, you too. You deserve it. And the best place to start? Exactly where you're at right now. So, get yourself a cup of a fun beverage of your choice, clear some space around you, and get started on the next page. Now, it might feel like you are alone in this, but please know that you are just one of many who are taking time out to design their new tomorrow — each with their own hopes and dreams for the future. So, let's get started, shall we?

I'm in your corner! Cheers!   *Krystal*

Commit to Your Journey

THE CHOICE TO CHANGE

Since you were a child, you have been learning who you are based on the people around you, the places you've lived, and the life experiences you have had. All these things shaped you to be who you are today. And you know, the tough experiences or memories... yes those shaped us as well. We must own and honor all parts of us, even the tough or rough sides. The difference is, we are not defined by our past. We have the power to define and design the life we desire. Right now, with what you have got! Now, you are about to embark on a whole new chapter in your life. Some things will stay the same, but some things will have to change. As you level up your life and your goals, your goals and actions must shift to align to your deepest desires.

You will experience life's beauty, challenges, chaos, and create memories. You will celebrate every step of the way. In this moment, you've been given a gift — the gift to decide. You get to decide what you will do, how you will live, and who you will become. It's a new start — a first step in the next leg of your journey. Sure, things could stay the same. You could stop here, refuse to grow, and keep living life inside of your comfort zone. But in this moment, with this breath, you have a chance to say yes. Not to yourself, but to the future woman that you are meant to be — the one who is waiting for you to step out, stand up, and commit to yourself — once and for all. So, let me ask you, are you ready for the next step?!

A Letter To Myself

··

Dear _____,

It's time. I am ready to let go of the old, commit to myself and embrace change. I believe that the world is transformed by the choices we make and I know that my life is important. My words, thoughts and actions are powerful.

So I am open to becoming more _____ and choose to do more _____. I am ready to commit to releasing my old stories about who I am and what I am capable of because _____.

This year I am going to be _____ I'm going to spend more time with _____, _____, _____ doing things like _____, _____, & _____.

I am also going to devote myself to spending less time doing things that waste my precious time like _____, _____, & _____ because they make me feel _____, _____, & _____.

The top three things that are important to me are.....
1.
2.
3.
...and I am ready to make them a priority in my life. No matter what.

One last thing: I love you and appreciate you _____, because of all of the amazing things you have made it through and all the incredible things you have accomplished. Especially that time you _____.

I wish for you a life worth living, my friend. And I'll be here with you, until the end.

With love,

HOW IT WORKS
MONTHLY

Fill in the simple-to-use monthly goals and gratitude, then
reflect at the end of each month on your progress! Get creative!!
YOU GET TO DESIGN THE LIFE YOU DESIRE!

WRITE THE MONTH
AND YEAR HERE

WRITE
YOUR BIG
GOALS FOR
THE MONTH
HERE

WRITE 5 PEOPLE OR
THINGS YOU'RE
GRATEFUL FOR HERE

WRITE HOW YOU
WILL SHOW UP
FOR THOSE WHO
NEED YOU THIS
MONTH HERE

LIST THE THINGS THAT YOU
MUST DO TO ACHIEVE YOUR
GOALS THIS MONTH

Monthly Intentions
THE FIRST MONTH

Date April 2022

GOALS FOR THE MONTH
- Get promoted
- Start the business
- Finish a 5k!
- Publish a book
- Book a vacation

THE "I GET TO" LIST

WHO/WHAT AM I GRATEFUL FOR?
- My family
- My Coach
- My planner!
- Quiet cup of coffee
- My Courage!

HOW WILL I SHOW UP THIS
MONTH FOR MY PEOPLE?

Be more present

KRYSTALORECREWS.COM | THE CREWS COACH ©2021

HOW IT WORKS
MONTHLY

Reflect on your monthly goals and gratitude, then
document your progress! Honor your wins and be honest with yourself!
Design a plan for staying on track for next month!

MONTHLY REFLECTION
PAGE: HOW DID YOU
DO?? BE HONEST!

Monthly Review
THE FIRST MONTH

Date **April 2022**

Instructions: rate your life across all 8 pillars from 1-5.

3 Health & Fitness   4 Career   3 Personal Growth   3 Spirituality
2 Relationships   3 Social & Liesure   2 Quality of Life   1 Finances

CELEBRATING WINS

Share your favorite memories this month.

Family outing to park

What are your big wins for this month?

I worked out 5x each week!

How did you celebrate them?

I will go buy new fun tank top!

OVERCOMING OBSTACLES

What "life situation" came up this month that may have derailed you?

Husband is sick

How will you overcome it or manage the obstacle?

Ask neighbor for help

What would your future self tell you to do today to start momentum?

Commit to self care

WHAT DO YOU WANT TO IMPROVE?

1. Be more present
2. Ask for help
3. Get better sleep

HOW DO YOU FEEL IN YOUR BODY?

Grounded and calm

WHO HELD YOU ACCOUNTABLE?

My coach & friend___

KRYSTALORECREWS.COM | THE CREWS COACH ©2021

HOW IT WORKS
WEEKLY

Simply fill in the simple-to-use weekly intentions and review pages.
Schedule time for yourself to plan your week out ahead of time!
Don't forget to schedule YOURSELF in there too!

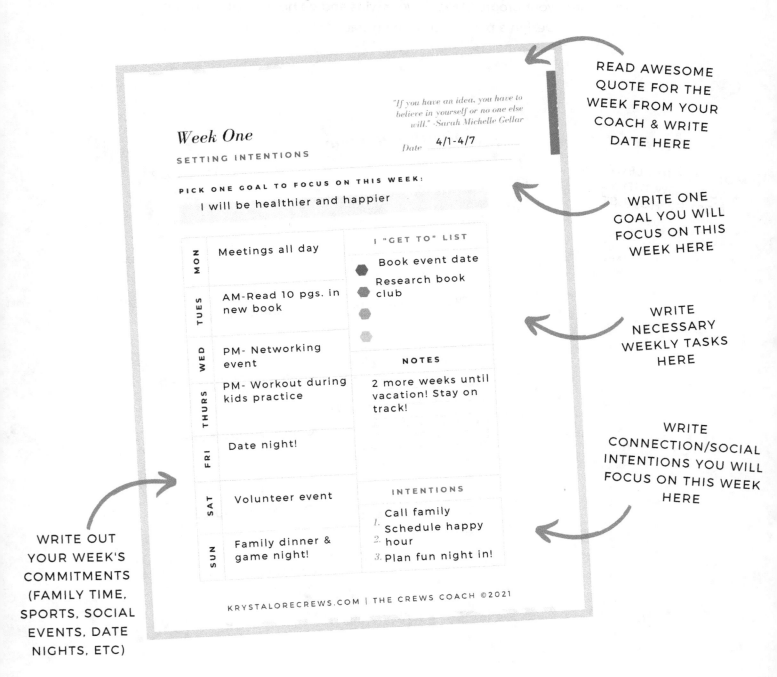

READ AWESOME QUOTE FOR THE WEEK FROM YOUR COACH & WRITE DATE HERE

WRITE ONE GOAL YOU WILL FOCUS ON THIS WEEK HERE

WRITE NECESSARY WEEKLY TASKS HERE

WRITE CONNECTION/SOCIAL INTENTIONS YOU WILL FOCUS ON THIS WEEK HERE

WRITE OUT YOUR WEEK'S COMMITMENTS (FAMILY TIME, SPORTS, SOCIAL EVENTS, DATE NIGHTS, ETC)

HOW IT WORKS
WEEKLY

Reflect on your weekly goals, fitness, nutrition, and intentions, then document your progress! Honor your wins and be honest with yourself! Design a plan for staying on track for next month!

WEEKLY REVIEW & REFLECTION... BE HONEST!

SCORE AND RESPOND TO YOUR HABITS

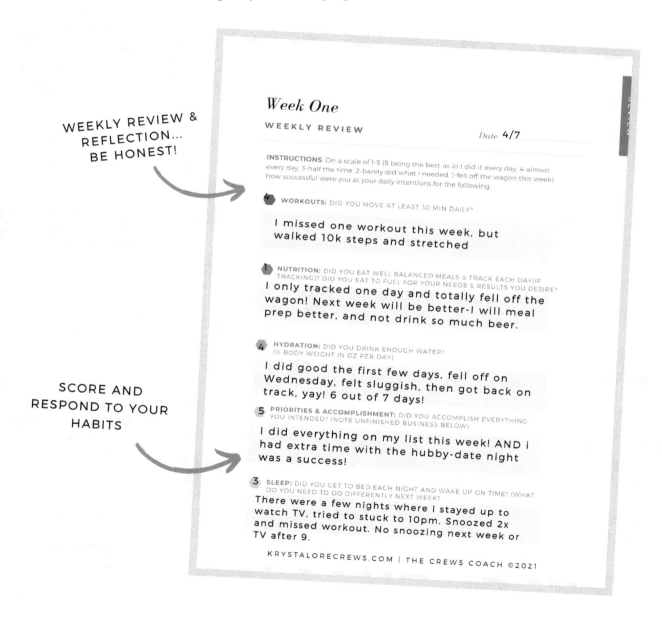

Week One
WEEKLY REVIEW

Date **4/7**

INSTRUCTIONS: On a scale of 1-5 (5 being the best-as in I did it every day, 4-almost every day, 3-half the time, 2-barely did what I needed, 1-fell off the wagon this week) how successful were you at your daily intentions for the following:

4 **WORKOUTS:** DID YOU MOVE AT LEAST 30 MIN DAILY?

I missed one workout this week, but walked 10k steps and stretched

1 **NUTRITION:** DID YOU EAT WELL BALANCED MEALS & TRACK EACH DAY(IF TRACKING)? DID YOU EAT TO FUEL FOR YOUR NEEDS & RESULTS YOU DESIRE?

I only tracked one day and totally fell off the wagon! Next week will be better-I will meal prep better, and not drink so much beer.

4 **HYDRATION:** DID YOU DRINK ENOUGH WATER? (½ BODY WEIGHT IN OZ PER DAY)

I did good the first few days, fell off on Wednesday, felt sluggish, then got back on track, yay! 6 out of 7 days!

5 **PRIORITIES & ACCOMPLISHMENT:** DID YOU ACCOMPLISH EVERYTHING YOU INTENDED? (NOTE UNFINISHED BUSINESS BELOW)

I did everything on my list this week! AND i had extra time with the hubby-date night was a success!

3 **SLEEP:** DID YOU GET TO BED EACH NIGHT AND WAKE UP ON TIME? (WHAT DO YOU NEED TO DO DIFFERENTLY NEXT WEEK?

There were a few nights where I stayed up to watch TV, tried to stuck to 10pm. Snoozed 2x and missed workout. No snoozing next week or TV after 9.

KRYSTALORECREWS.COM | THE CREWS COACH ©2021

HOW IT WORKS
DAILY MORNING

Fill in the simple-to-use intentions, gratitude and journaling pages every single day! Take some time each night to reflect and score yourself. Be intentional and realistic! Stick to your plan! Make necessary adjustments to meet your goals, and gain momentum towards results! Results are FUN!

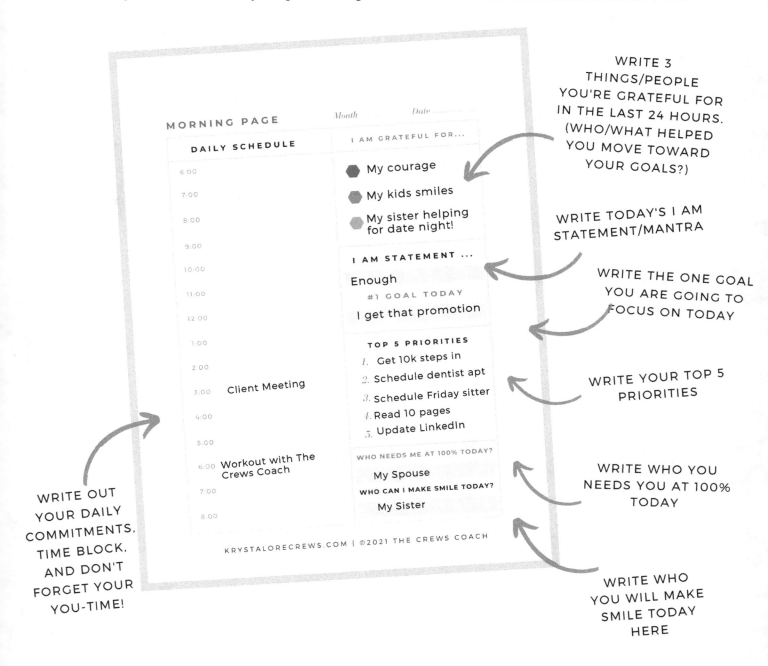

WRITE 3 THINGS/PEOPLE YOU'RE GRATEFUL FOR IN THE LAST 24 HOURS. (WHO/WHAT HELPED YOU MOVE TOWARD YOUR GOALS?)

WRITE TODAY'S I AM STATEMENT/MANTRA

WRITE THE ONE GOAL YOU ARE GOING TO FOCUS ON TODAY

WRITE YOUR TOP 5 PRIORITIES

WRITE WHO YOU NEEDS YOU AT 100% TODAY

WRITE WHO YOU WILL MAKE SMILE TODAY HERE

WRITE OUT YOUR DAILY COMMITMENTS, TIME BLOCK, AND DON'T FORGET YOUR YOU-TIME!

Content shown in the morning page:

MORNING PAGE — Month ___ Date ___

DAILY SCHEDULE
- 6:00
- 7:00
- 8:00
- 9:00
- 10:00
- 11:00
- 12:00
- 1:00
- 2:00
- 3:00 Client Meeting
- 4:00
- 5:00
- 6:00 Workout with The Crews Coach
- 7:00
- 8:00

I AM GRATEFUL FOR...
- My courage
- My kids smiles
- My sister helping for date night!

I AM STATEMENT ...
Enough

#1 GOAL TODAY
I get that promotion

TOP 5 PRIORITIES
1. Get 10k steps in
2. Schedule dentist apt
3. Schedule Friday sitter
4. Read 10 pages
5. Update LinkedIn

WHO NEEDS ME AT 100% TODAY?
My Spouse

WHO CAN I MAKE SMILE TODAY?
My Sister

KRYSTALORECREWS.COM | ©2021 THE CREWS COACH

HOW IT WORKS
DAILY EVENING

Simply print out the following pages and then fill in the simple-to-use intentions, gratitude and journaling pages every single day! Take some time each night to reflect and score yourself. Make necessary adjustments to meet your goals, and gain momentum towards results! Results are FUN!

COMPLETE EVENING REFLECION PAGES... BE HONEST WITH YOURSELF!

CELEBRATE ALL OF YOUR WINS AND CELEBRATIONS FOR THE DAY! BIG OR SMALL!

SCORE YOURSELF ON HOW ACCOMPLISHED YOU WERE TODAY! 5 BEING MOST PRODUCTIVE!

WRITE A CHECK MARK OR SMILEY FACE IF YOU COMPLETED YOUR HYDRATION & WORKOUT GOAL. IF YOU DIDN'T PUT A "0" OR SAD FACE

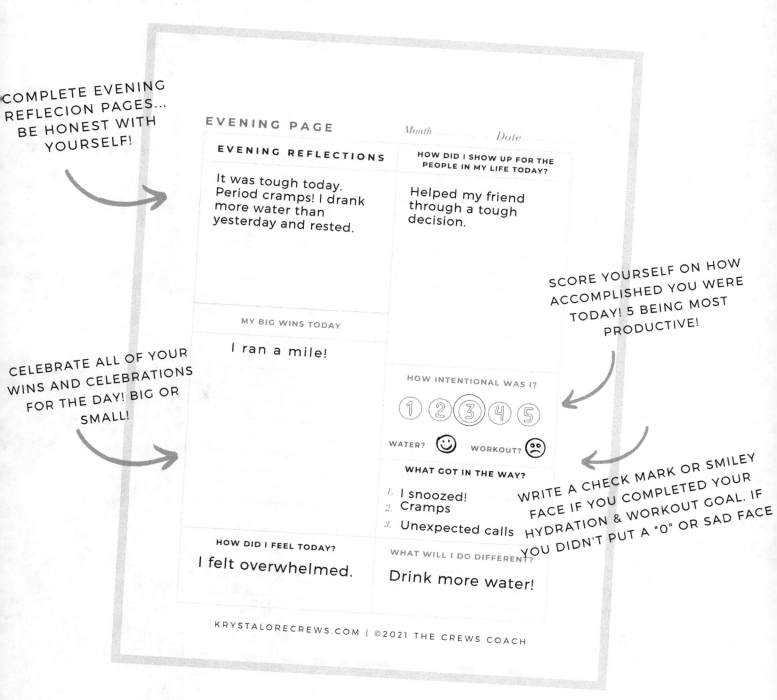

EVENING PAGE   *Month*   *Date*

EVENING REFLECTIONS

It was tough today. Period cramps! I drank more water than yesterday and rested.

HOW DID I SHOW UP FOR THE PEOPLE IN MY LIFE TODAY?

Helped my friend through a tough decision.

MY BIG WINS TODAY

I ran a mile!

HOW INTENTIONAL WAS I?

① ② ③ ④ ⑤

WATER? ☺   WORKOUT? ☹

WHAT GOT IN THE WAY?

1. I snoozed!
2. Cramps
3. Unexpected calls

HOW DID I FEEL TODAY?

I felt overwhelmed.

WHAT WILL I DO DIFFERENT?

Drink more water!

KRYSTALORECREWS.COM | ©2021 THE CREWS COACH

Dream Day Ritual

You know in movies when the main character rolls out of bed to the sound of their alarm clock, loathing the daily grind, their job, their relationship, and end up miserable and unhealthy?? Annoying right? I feel the same way. But you know what? It doesn't have to be that way. In fact, it shouldn't be. Your life shouldn't be something that you have to be forced into. And even when times are tough, there should always be something to look forward to. That perfect cup of coffee, the call from a friend, the sound of the birds outside your window or the feeling you get when you finally hit your goal. Most of us have been told that life is hard and it's supposed to be. That there isn't anything worth looking forward to. And to simply just get by. But I believe so much more is possible for us all. And I know you do to. So I want you to take some time to write out your dream day. Who would you be spending it with? What would you do? Where would you live? How would you dress? Imagine what it could be like, so you can start to make little changes to create that for yourself. One day at a time.

Dream Day Ritual

UNCOVER WHAT REALLY MATTERS

Take deep breath! Before you begin, I want you to close your eyes and think about what it is you really want. Yes, what do YOU want? Write down the details of what your ideal day would look like and feel like. Be as vivid and descriptive as you can!

Setting Your Goals

DEFINE YOUR INTENTIONS

Even if it doesn't quite feel like it yet, there is a reason why you want what you want. Which is why you should never EVER listen to anyone else tell you what that is. Your dreams and desires are unique. And they should be. Because nobody else knows what is in your heart.

So it's time to give up the fight. That never ending race to the an invisible finish line. That you will never live up to. Those unrealistic and even harmful expectations that other people have for you and even those you have for yourself.

Take some time to get clear on the goals you have for yourself. Don't let anyone stop you from dreaming big here. Write down what you want to feel, do and become in every area of your life. How do you want to feel? What do you want to do? And who do you want to become?

This is your chance to make those things happen, but first you have to write them down - so you can!

90 Day Goal Setting

REVIEW YOUR 8 PILLARS

This is the place to explore how you want to feel, what you want to do and who you want to become in the next 90 days of your life. Write down each of your goals in the following areas of your life corresponding to the 8 pillars. Try to visualize and capture the emotions you will feel once you accomplish your goal in each area. Score yourself as a benchmark 1-5, with 5 being the happiest you are in this part of your life.

HEALTH & FITNESS	CAREER
Rate out of 5: ☐	Rate out of 5: ☐

PERSONAL GROWTH	SPIRITUALITY
Rate out of 5: ☐	Rate out of 5: ☐

RELATIONSHIPS	SOCIAL & LEISURE
Rate out of 5: ☐	Rate out of 5: ☐

QUALITY OF LIFE	FINANCES
Rate out of 5: ☐	Rate out of 5: ☐

Month
ONE

Monthly Intentions

THE FIRST MONTH

Month _____ *Date* _____

GOALS FOR THE MONTH

⬣

⬣

⬣

⬣

⬣

WHO/WHAT AM I GRATEFUL FOR?

⬣

⬣

⬣

⬣

⬣

THE "I GET TO" LIST

☐ _____

☐ _____

☐ _____

☐ _____

☐ _____

☐ _____

☐ _____

☐ _____

☐ _____

☐ _____

HOW WILL I SHOW UP THIS MONTH FOR MY PEOPLE?

Week One

SETTING INTENTIONS

"You are in control of your body, life, and results. Don't let your mind bully your body." -Krystalore Crews

Month _____ *Date* _____

PICK ONE GOAL TO FOCUS ON THIS WEEK:

MON		**I "GET TO" LIST**
TUES		⬡
		⬡
WED		⬡
		⬡
THURS		**NOTES**
FRI		
SAT		**SOCIAL INTENTIONS**
SUN		*1.*
		2.
		3.

Notes, Quotes, and Relfections

MORNING PAGE

Day _____ *Date* _____

DAILY SCHEDULE	I AM GRATEFUL FOR...
6:00	
7:00	
8:00	
9:00	
10:00	**I AM STATEMENT ...**
11:00	
12:00	**#1 GOAL TODAY**
1:00	
2:00	**TOP 5 PRIORITIES**
3:00	*1.*
	2.
4:00	*3.*
	4.
5:00	*5.*
6:00	**WHO NEEDS ME AT 100% TODAY?**
7:00	**WHO CAN I MAKE SMILE TODAY?**
8:00	

EVENING PAGE

Day _____ *Date* _____

EVENING REFLECTIONS

HOW DID I SHOW UP FOR THE PEOPLE IN MY LIFE TODAY?

MY BIG WINS TODAY

HOW INTENTIONAL WAS I?

(1) (2) (3) (4) (5)

WATER? ☐   WORKOUT? ☐

WHAT GOT IN THE WAY?

1.
2.
3.

HOW DID I FEEL TODAY?

WHAT WILL I DO DIFFERENT?

MORNING PAGE

Day ———————— *Date* ————————

DAILY SCHEDULE	I AM GRATEFUL FOR...
6:00	
7:00	
8:00	
9:00	
10:00	**I AM STATEMENT ...**
11:00	
12:00	**#1 GOAL TODAY**
1:00	
2:00	**TOP 5 PRIORITIES**
	1.
3:00	*2.*
	3.
4:00	*4.*
5:00	*5.*
6:00	**WHO NEEDS ME AT 100% TODAY?**
7:00	**WHO CAN I MAKE SMILE TODAY?**
8:00	

EVENING PAGE

Day ———————— *Date* ————————

EVENING REFLECTIONS

HOW DID I SHOW UP FOR THE PEOPLE IN MY LIFE TODAY?

MY BIG WINS TODAY

HOW INTENTIONAL WAS I?

(1) (2) (3) (4) (5)

WATER? ☐   WORKOUT? ☐

WHAT GOT IN THE WAY?

1.

2.

3.

HOW DID I FEEL TODAY?

WHAT WILL I DO DIFFERENT?

MORNING PAGE

Day ———————— *Date* ————————

DAILY SCHEDULE	I AM GRATEFUL FOR...
6:00	
7:00	
8:00	
9:00	
10:00	**I AM STATEMENT ...**
11:00	**#1 GOAL TODAY**
12:00	
1:00	**TOP 5 PRIORITIES**
2:00	*1.*
3:00	*2.*
	3.
4:00	*4.*
5:00	*5.*
6:00	**WHO NEEDS ME AT 100% TODAY?**
7:00	**WHO CAN I MAKE SMILE TODAY?**
8:00	

EVENING PAGE

Day ———————— *Date* ————————

EVENING REFLECTIONS	HOW DID I SHOW UP FOR THE PEOPLE IN MY LIFE TODAY?

MY BIG WINS TODAY

HOW INTENTIONAL WAS I?

① ② ③ ④ ⑤

WATER? ☐   WORKOUT? ☐

WHAT GOT IN THE WAY?

1.
2.
3.

HOW DID I FEEL TODAY?

WHAT WILL I DO DIFFERENT?

MORNING PAGE

Day ———————— *Date* ————————

DAILY SCHEDULE	I AM GRATEFUL FOR...
6:00	
7:00	
8:00	
9:00	
10:00	**I AM STATEMENT ...**
11:00	**#1 GOAL TODAY**
12:00	
1:00	**TOP 5 PRIORITIES**
2:00	*1.*
3:00	*2.*
	3.
4:00	*4.*
5:00	*5.*
6:00	**WHO NEEDS ME AT 100% TODAY?**
7:00	**WHO CAN I MAKE SMILE TODAY?**
8:00	

EVENING PAGE

Day ———— *Date*

EVENING REFLECTIONS

MY BIG WINS TODAY

HOW DID I FEEL TODAY?

HOW DID I SHOW UP FOR THE PEOPLE IN MY LIFE TODAY?

HOW INTENTIONAL WAS I?

① ② ③ ④ ⑤

WATER? ☐   WORKOUT? ☐

WHAT GOT IN THE WAY?

1.

2.

3.

WHAT WILL I DO DIFFERENT?

MORNING PAGE

Day ———————— *Date* ————————

DAILY SCHEDULE	I AM GRATEFUL FOR...
6:00	
7:00	
8:00	
9:00	

I AM STATEMENT ...

#1 GOAL TODAY

DAILY SCHEDULE (cont.)	TOP 5 PRIORITIES
10:00	
11:00	
12:00	1.
1:00	2.
2:00	3.
3:00	4.
4:00	5.
5:00	

WHO NEEDS ME AT 100% TODAY?

WHO CAN I MAKE SMILE TODAY?

6:00	
7:00	
8:00	

EVENING PAGE

Day _____ *Date* _____

EVENING REFLECTIONS

HOW DID I SHOW UP FOR THE PEOPLE IN MY LIFE TODAY?

MY BIG WINS TODAY

HOW INTENTIONAL WAS I?

① ② ③ ④ ⑤

WATER? ☐   WORKOUT? ☐

WHAT GOT IN THE WAY?

1.

2.

3.

HOW DID I FEEL TODAY?

WHAT WILL I DO DIFFERENT?

MORNING PAGE

Day ——————— *Date* ———————

DAILY SCHEDULE	I AM GRATEFUL FOR...
6:00	
7:00	
8:00	
9:00	
10:00	**I AM STATEMENT ...**
11:00	
12:00	**#1 GOAL TODAY**
1:00	
2:00	**TOP 5 PRIORITIES**
	1.
3:00	*2.*
	3.
4:00	*4.*
5:00	*5.*
6:00	**WHO NEEDS ME AT 100% TODAY?**
7:00	
	WHO CAN I MAKE SMILE TODAY?
8:00	

EVENING PAGE

Day ———————————— *Date* ————————————

EVENING REFLECTIONS	HOW DID I SHOW UP FOR THE PEOPLE IN MY LIFE TODAY?

MY BIG WINS TODAY

HOW INTENTIONAL WAS I?

① ② ③ ④ ⑤

WATER? ☐   WORKOUT? ☐

WHAT GOT IN THE WAY?

1.

2.

3.

HOW DID I FEEL TODAY?

WHAT WILL I DO DIFFERENT?

MORNING PAGE

Day _____ *Date* _____

DAILY SCHEDULE	I AM GRATEFUL FOR...
6:00	
7:00	
8:00	
9:00	
10:00	**I AM STATEMENT ...**
11:00	**#1 GOAL TODAY**
12:00	
1:00	**TOP 5 PRIORITIES**
2:00	*1.*
3:00	*2.*
	3.
4:00	*4.*
5:00	*5.*
6:00	**WHO NEEDS ME AT 100% TODAY?**
7:00	**WHO CAN I MAKE SMILE TODAY?**
8:00	

EVENING PAGE

Day _____ *Date* _____

EVENING REFLECTIONS

MY BIG WINS TODAY

HOW DID I FEEL TODAY?

HOW DID I SHOW UP FOR THE PEOPLE IN MY LIFE TODAY?

HOW INTENTIONAL WAS I?

(1) (2) (3) (4) (5)

WATER? ☐   WORKOUT? ☐

WHAT GOT IN THE WAY?

1.

2.

3.

WHAT WILL I DO DIFFERENT?

Week One

WEEKLY REVIEW

Month _____ *Date* _____

INSTRUCTIONS: On a scale of 1-5 (5 being the best-as in I did it every day, 4-almost every day, 3-half the time, 2-barely did what I needed, 1-fell off the wagon this week) how successful were you at your daily intentions for the following:

⬢ **WORKOUTS:** DID YOU MOVE AT LEAST 30 MIN DAILY?

⬢ **NUTRITION:** DID YOU EAT WELL BALANCED MEALS & TRACK EACH DAY(IF TRACKING)? DID YOU EAT TO FUEL FOR YOUR NEEDS & RESULTS YOU DESIRE?

⬢ **HYDRATION:** DID YOU DRINK ENOUGH WATER?
(½ BODY WEIGHT IN OZ PER DAY)

⬢ **PRIORITIES & ACCOMPLISHMENT:** DID YOU ACCOMPLISH EVERYTHING YOU INTENDED? (NOTE UNFINISHED BUSINESS BELOW)

⬢ **SLEEP:** DID YOU GET TO BED EACH NIGHT AND WAKE UP ON TIME? (WHAT DO YOU NEED TO DO DIFFERENTLY NEXT WEEK?

Week In Reflection

Yay! You showed up this week!! What were your biggest reflections, wins, memories, and challenges? How will you use this to fuel you forward into next week?

Week Two

SETTING INTENTIONS

Month _____ *Date* _____

PICK ONE GOAL TO FOCUS ON THIS WEEK:

MON	**I "GET TO" LIST**
TUES	
WED	
	NOTES
THURS	
FRI	
SAT	**SOCIAL INTENTIONS**
SUN	1.
	2.
	3.

Notes, Quotes, and Relfections

MORNING PAGE

Day _____ *Date* _____

DAILY SCHEDULE	I AM GRATEFUL FOR...
6:00	
7:00	
8:00	
9:00	
10:00	**I AM STATEMENT ...**
11:00	
12:00	**#1 GOAL TODAY**
1:00	
2:00	**TOP 5 PRIORITIES**
3:00	*1.*
4:00	*2.*
5:00	*3.*
	4.
	5.
6:00	**WHO NEEDS ME AT 100% TODAY?**
7:00	
8:00	**WHO CAN I MAKE SMILE TODAY?**

EVENING PAGE

Day ———————— *Date* ————————

EVENING REFLECTIONS

HOW DID I SHOW UP FOR THE PEOPLE IN MY LIFE TODAY?

MY BIG WINS TODAY

HOW INTENTIONAL WAS I?

① ② ③ ④ ⑤

WATER? ☐   WORKOUT? ☐

WHAT GOT IN THE WAY?

1.

2.

3.

HOW DID I FEEL TODAY?

WHAT WILL I DO DIFFERENT?

MORNING PAGE

Day _____ *Date* _____

DAILY SCHEDULE	I AM GRATEFUL FOR...
6:00	
7:00	
8:00	
9:00	**I AM STATEMENT ...**
10:00	
11:00	**#1 GOAL TODAY**
12:00	
1:00	**TOP 5 PRIORITIES**
2:00	*1.*
3:00	*2.*
	3.
4:00	*4.*
5:00	*5.*
6:00	**WHO NEEDS ME AT 100% TODAY?**
7:00	**WHO CAN I MAKE SMILE TODAY?**
8:00	

EVENING PAGE

Day ——————— *Date* ———————

EVENING REFLECTIONS

HOW DID I SHOW UP FOR THE PEOPLE IN MY LIFE TODAY?

MY BIG WINS TODAY

HOW INTENTIONAL WAS I?

① ② ③ ④ ⑤

WATER? ☐   WORKOUT? ☐

WHAT GOT IN THE WAY?

1.

2.

3.

HOW DID I FEEL TODAY?

WHAT WILL I DO DIFFERENT?

MORNING PAGE

Day ———————— *Date* ————————

DAILY SCHEDULE	I AM GRATEFUL FOR...
6:00	
7:00	
8:00	
9:00	
10:00	**I AM STATEMENT ...**
11:00	**#1 GOAL TODAY**
12:00	
1:00	**TOP 5 PRIORITIES**
2:00	*1.*
3:00	*2.*
	3.
4:00	*4.*
5:00	*5.*
6:00	**WHO NEEDS ME AT 100% TODAY?**
7:00	**WHO CAN I MAKE SMILE TODAY?**
8:00	

EVENING PAGE

Day ——————— *Date* ———————

EVENING REFLECTIONS

MY BIG WINS TODAY

HOW DID I SHOW UP FOR THE PEOPLE IN MY LIFE TODAY?

HOW INTENTIONAL WAS I?

① ② ③ ④ ⑤

WATER? ☐　　WORKOUT? ☐

WHAT GOT IN THE WAY?

1. ———————————

2. ———————————

3. ———————————

HOW DID I FEEL TODAY?

WHAT WILL I DO DIFFERENT?

MORNING PAGE

Day _____ *Date* _____

DAILY SCHEDULE	I AM GRATEFUL FOR...
6:00	
7:00	
8:00	
9:00	
10:00	**I AM STATEMENT ...**
11:00	
12:00	**#1 GOAL TODAY**
1:00	
2:00	**TOP 5 PRIORITIES**
3:00	*1.*
4:00	*2.*
5:00	*3.*
6:00	*4.*
7:00	*5.*
8:00	**WHO NEEDS ME AT 100% TODAY?**
	WHO CAN I MAKE SMILE TODAY?

EVENING PAGE

Day _____ *Date* _____

EVENING REFLECTIONS

HOW DID I SHOW UP FOR THE PEOPLE IN MY LIFE TODAY?

MY BIG WINS TODAY

HOW INTENTIONAL WAS I?

① ② ③ ④ ⑤

WATER? ☐   WORKOUT? ☐

WHAT GOT IN THE WAY?

1.
2.
3.

HOW DID I FEEL TODAY?

WHAT WILL I DO DIFFERENT?

MORNING PAGE

Day ———————— *Date* ————————

DAILY SCHEDULE	I AM GRATEFUL FOR...
6:00	
7:00	
8:00	
9:00	
10:00	**I AM STATEMENT ...**
11:00	
12:00	**#1 GOAL TODAY**
1:00	
2:00	**TOP 5 PRIORITIES**
3:00	*1.*
4:00	*2.*
5:00	*3.*
6:00	*4.*
7:00	*5.*
8:00	**WHO NEEDS ME AT 100% TODAY?**
	WHO CAN I MAKE SMILE TODAY?

EVENING PAGE

Day ————— *Date* —————

EVENING REFLECTIONS

HOW DID I SHOW UP FOR THE PEOPLE IN MY LIFE TODAY?

MY BIG WINS TODAY

HOW INTENTIONAL WAS I?

① ② ③ ④ ⑤

WATER? ☐   WORKOUT? ☐

WHAT GOT IN THE WAY?

1.

2.

3.

HOW DID I FEEL TODAY?

WHAT WILL I DO DIFFERENT?

MORNING PAGE

Day _____ *Date* _____

DAILY SCHEDULE	I AM GRATEFUL FOR...

DAILY SCHEDULE

6:00

7:00

8:00

9:00

10:00

11:00

12:00

1:00

2:00

3:00

4:00

5:00

6:00

7:00

8:00

I AM GRATEFUL FOR...

I AM STATEMENT ...

#1 GOAL TODAY

TOP 5 PRIORITIES

1.

2.

3.

4.

5.

WHO NEEDS ME AT 100% TODAY?

WHO CAN I MAKE SMILE TODAY?

EVENING PAGE

Day _____ *Date* _____

EVENING REFLECTIONS	HOW DID I SHOW UP FOR THE PEOPLE IN MY LIFE TODAY?

MY BIG WINS TODAY

HOW INTENTIONAL WAS I?

① ② ③ ④ ⑤

WATER? ☐   WORKOUT? ☐

WHAT GOT IN THE WAY?

1.
2.
3.

HOW DID I FEEL TODAY?

WHAT WILL I DO DIFFERENT?

MORNING PAGE

Day ——————— *Date* ———————

DAILY SCHEDULE	I AM GRATEFUL FOR...
6:00	
7:00	
8:00	
9:00	
10:00	**I AM STATEMENT ...**
11:00	
12:00	**#1 GOAL TODAY**
1:00	
2:00	**TOP 5 PRIORITIES**
3:00	*1.*
	2.
4:00	*3.*
	4.
5:00	*5.*
6:00	**WHO NEEDS ME AT 100% TODAY?**
7:00	
	WHO CAN I MAKE SMILE TODAY?
8:00	

EVENING PAGE

Day ——————— *Date* ———————

EVENING REFLECTIONS

HOW DID I SHOW UP FOR THE PEOPLE IN MY LIFE TODAY?

MY BIG WINS TODAY

HOW INTENTIONAL WAS I?

① ② ③ ④ ⑤

WATER? ☐   WORKOUT? ☐

WHAT GOT IN THE WAY?

1.

2.

3.

HOW DID I FEEL TODAY?

WHAT WILL I DO DIFFERENT?

Week Two

WEEKLY REVIEW

Month _____ *Date* _____

INSTRUCTIONS: On a scale of 1-5 (5 being the best-as in I did it every day, 4-almost every day, 3-half the time, 2-barely did what I needed, 1-fell off the wagon this week) how successful were you at your daily intentions for the following:

WORKOUTS: DID YOU MOVE AT LEAST 30 MIN DAILY?

NUTRITION: DID YOU EAT WELL BALANCED MEALS & TRACK EACH DAY(IF TRACKING)? DID YOU EAT TO FUEL FOR YOUR NEEDS & RESULTS YOU DESIRE?

HYDRATION: DID YOU DRINK ENOUGH WATER?
(½ BODY WEIGHT IN OZ PER DAY)

PRIORITIES & ACCOMPLISHMENT: DID YOU ACCOMPLISH EVERYTHING YOU INTENDED? (NOTE UNFINISHED BUSINESS BELOW)

SLEEP: DID YOU GET TO BED EACH NIGHT AND WAKE UP ON TIME? (WHAT DO YOU NEED TO DO DIFFERENTLY NEXT WEEK?

Week In Reflection

Yay! You showed up this week!! What were your biggest reflections, wins, memories, and challenges? How will you use this to fuel you forward into next week?

Week Three

SETTING INTENTIONS

"Crews Beyond Limits is not a fad, it's a lifestyle." -Krystalore Crews

Month _____ *Date* _____

PICK ONE GOAL TO FOCUS ON THIS WEEK:

		I "GET TO" LIST
MON		
TUES		⬡
		⬡
WED		⬡
		⬡
THURS		**NOTES**
FRI		
SAT		**SOCIAL INTENTIONS**
SUN		*1.* *2.* *3.*

Notes, Quotes, and Relfections

MORNING PAGE

Day _____ *Date* _____

DAILY SCHEDULE	I AM GRATEFUL FOR...
6:00	
7:00	
8:00	
9:00	
10:00	**I AM STATEMENT ...**
11:00	
12:00	**#1 GOAL TODAY**
1:00	
2:00	**TOP 5 PRIORITIES**
	1.
3:00	*2.*
	3.
4:00	*4.*
5:00	*5.*
6:00	**WHO NEEDS ME AT 100% TODAY?**
7:00	**WHO CAN I MAKE SMILE TODAY?**
8:00	

EVENING PAGE

Day _____ *Date* _____

EVENING REFLECTIONS

HOW DID I SHOW UP FOR THE PEOPLE IN MY LIFE TODAY?

MY BIG WINS TODAY

HOW INTENTIONAL WAS I?

(1) (2) (3) (4) (5)

WATER? ☐   WORKOUT? ☐

WHAT GOT IN THE WAY?

1.
2.
3.

HOW DID I FEEL TODAY?

WHAT WILL I DO DIFFERENT?

MORNING PAGE

Day _____ *Date* _____

DAILY SCHEDULE	I AM GRATEFUL FOR...
6:00	
7:00	
8:00	
9:00	
10:00	**I AM STATEMENT ...**
11:00	
12:00	**#1 GOAL TODAY**
1:00	
2:00	**TOP 5 PRIORITIES**
3:00	*1.*
	2.
4:00	*3.*
	4.
5:00	*5.*
6:00	**WHO NEEDS ME AT 100% TODAY?**
7:00	**WHO CAN I MAKE SMILE TODAY?**
8:00	

EVENING PAGE

Day ——————— *Date* ———————

EVENING REFLECTIONS

MY BIG WINS TODAY

HOW DID I FEEL TODAY?

HOW DID I SHOW UP FOR THE PEOPLE IN MY LIFE TODAY?

HOW INTENTIONAL WAS I?

(1) (2) (3) (4) (5)

WATER? ☐   WORKOUT? ☐

WHAT GOT IN THE WAY?

1.

2.

3.

WHAT WILL I DO DIFFERENT?

MORNING PAGE

Day —————— *Date* ——————

DAILY SCHEDULE

6:00

7:00

8:00

9:00

10:00

11:00

12:00

1:00

2:00

3:00

4:00

5:00

6:00

7:00

8:00

I AM GRATEFUL FOR...

I AM STATEMENT ...

#1 GOAL TODAY

TOP 5 PRIORITIES

1.

2.

3.

4.

5.

WHO NEEDS ME AT 100% TODAY?

WHO CAN I MAKE SMILE TODAY?

EVENING PAGE

Day _____ *Date* _____

EVENING REFLECTIONS	HOW DID I SHOW UP FOR THE PEOPLE IN MY LIFE TODAY?

MY BIG WINS TODAY

HOW INTENTIONAL WAS I?

① ② ③ ④ ⑤

WATER? ☐   WORKOUT? ☐

WHAT GOT IN THE WAY?

1.

2.

3.

HOW DID I FEEL TODAY?

WHAT WILL I DO DIFFERENT?

MORNING PAGE

Day _____ *Date* _____

DAILY SCHEDULE

6:00

7:00

8:00

9:00

10:00

11:00

12:00

1:00

2:00

3:00

4:00

5:00

6:00

7:00

8:00

I AM GRATEFUL FOR...

I AM STATEMENT ...

#1 GOAL TODAY

TOP 5 PRIORITIES

1.

2.

3.

4.

5.

WHO NEEDS ME AT 100% TODAY?

WHO CAN I MAKE SMILE TODAY?

EVENING PAGE

Day ———————— *Date* ————————

EVENING REFLECTIONS	HOW DID I SHOW UP FOR THE PEOPLE IN MY LIFE TODAY?

MY BIG WINS TODAY

HOW INTENTIONAL WAS I?

1 2 3 4 5

WATER? ☐   WORKOUT? ☐

WHAT GOT IN THE WAY?

1.

2.

3.

HOW DID I FEEL TODAY?

WHAT WILL I DO DIFFERENT?

MORNING PAGE

Day ———— *Date* ————

DAILY SCHEDULE	I AM GRATEFUL FOR...
6:00	
7:00	
8:00	
9:00	

I AM STATEMENT ...

#1 GOAL TODAY

TOP 5 PRIORITIES

1.

2.

3.

4.

5.

WHO NEEDS ME AT 100% TODAY?

WHO CAN I MAKE SMILE TODAY?

Daily schedule times: 10:00, 11:00, 12:00, 1:00, 2:00, 3:00, 4:00, 5:00, 6:00, 7:00, 8:00

EVENING PAGE

Day _____ *Date* _____

EVENING REFLECTIONS

HOW DID I SHOW UP FOR THE PEOPLE IN MY LIFE TODAY?

MY BIG WINS TODAY

HOW INTENTIONAL WAS I?

① ② ③ ④ ⑤

WATER? ☐   WORKOUT? ☐

WHAT GOT IN THE WAY?

1.

2.

3.

HOW DID I FEEL TODAY?

WHAT WILL I DO DIFFERENT?

MORNING PAGE

Day ——————— *Date* ———————

DAILY SCHEDULE	I AM GRATEFUL FOR...
6:00	
7:00	
8:00	
9:00	
10:00	**I AM STATEMENT ...**
11:00	**#1 GOAL TODAY**
12:00	
1:00	
2:00	**TOP 5 PRIORITIES**
2:00	*1.*
3:00	*2.*
	3.
4:00	*4.*
5:00	*5.*
6:00	**WHO NEEDS ME AT 100% TODAY?**
7:00	**WHO CAN I MAKE SMILE TODAY?**
8:00	

EVENING PAGE

Day ———— *Date* ————

EVENING REFLECTIONS

MY BIG WINS TODAY

HOW DID I FEEL TODAY?

HOW DID I SHOW UP FOR THE PEOPLE IN MY LIFE TODAY?

HOW INTENTIONAL WAS I?

1 2 3 4 5

WATER? ☐   WORKOUT? ☐

WHAT GOT IN THE WAY?

1.

2.

3.

WHAT WILL I DO DIFFERENT?

MORNING PAGE

Day ——————— *Date* ———————

DAILY SCHEDULE	I AM GRATEFUL FOR...
6:00	
7:00	
8:00	
9:00	
10:00	**I AM STATEMENT ...**
11:00	**#1 GOAL TODAY**
12:00	
1:00	**TOP 5 PRIORITIES**
2:00	*1.*
3:00	*2.*
	3.
4:00	*4.*
5:00	*5.*
6:00	**WHO NEEDS ME AT 100% TODAY?**
7:00	**WHO CAN I MAKE SMILE TODAY?**
8:00	

EVENING PAGE

Day ———————— *Date* ————————

EVENING REFLECTIONS	HOW DID I SHOW UP FOR THE PEOPLE IN MY LIFE TODAY?

MY BIG WINS TODAY

HOW INTENTIONAL WAS I?

① ② ③ ④ ⑤

WATER? ☐ WORKOUT? ☐

WHAT GOT IN THE WAY?

1. _____
2. _____
3. _____

HOW DID I FEEL TODAY?

WHAT WILL I DO DIFFERENT?

Week Three

WEEKLY REVIEW

Month _____ *Date* _____

INSTRUCTIONS: On a scale of 1-5 (5 being the best-as in I did it every day, 4-almost every day, 3-half the time, 2-barely did what I needed, 1-fell off the wagon this week) how successful were you at your daily intentions for the following:

WORKOUTS: DID YOU MOVE AT LEAST 30 MIN DAILY?

NUTRITION: DID YOU EAT WELL BALANCED MEALS & TRACK EACH DAY(IF TRACKING)? DID YOU EAT TO FUEL FOR YOUR NEEDS & RESULTS YOU DESIRE?

HYDRATION: DID YOU DRINK ENOUGH WATER?
(½ BODY WEIGHT IN OZ PER DAY)

PRIORITIES & ACCOMPLISHMENT: DID YOU ACCOMPLISH EVERYTHING YOU INTENDED? (NOTE UNFINISHED BUSINESS BELOW)

SLEEP: DID YOU GET TO BED EACH NIGHT AND WAKE UP ON TIME? (WHAT DO YOU NEED TO DO DIFFERENTLY NEXT WEEK?

Week In Reflection

Yay! You showed up this week!! What were your biggest reflections, wins, memories, and challenges? How will you use this to fuel you forward into next week?

Week Four

SETTING INTENTIONS

Month _____ *Date* _____

PICK ONE GOAL TO FOCUS ON THIS WEEK:

MON	
TUES	
WED	
THURS	
FRI	
SAT	
SUN	

I "GET TO" LIST

NOTES

SOCIAL INTENTIONS

1.

2.

3.

Notes, Quotes, and Relfections

MORNING PAGE

Day ———————— *Date* ————————

DAILY SCHEDULE	I AM GRATEFUL FOR...
6:00	
7:00	
8:00	
9:00	
10:00	**I AM STATEMENT ...**
11:00	
	#1 GOAL TODAY
12:00	
1:00	
2:00	**TOP 5 PRIORITIES**
	1.
3:00	*2.*
	3.
4:00	*4.*
5:00	*5.*
6:00	**WHO NEEDS ME AT 100% TODAY?**
7:00	
	WHO CAN I MAKE SMILE TODAY?
8:00	

EVENING PAGE

Day ———————— *Date* ————————

EVENING REFLECTIONS

HOW DID I SHOW UP FOR THE PEOPLE IN MY LIFE TODAY?

MY BIG WINS TODAY

HOW INTENTIONAL WAS I?

1 2 3 4 5

WATER? ☐   WORKOUT? ☐

WHAT GOT IN THE WAY?

1.
2.
3.

HOW DID I FEEL TODAY?

WHAT WILL I DO DIFFERENT?

MORNING PAGE

Day ——————— *Date* ———————

DAILY SCHEDULE	I AM GRATEFUL FOR...
6:00	
7:00	
8:00	
9:00	
10:00	**I AM STATEMENT ...**
11:00	**#1 GOAL TODAY**
12:00	
1:00	**TOP 5 PRIORITIES**
2:00	*1.*
3:00	*2.*
4:00	*3.*
	4.
5:00	*5.*
6:00	**WHO NEEDS ME AT 100% TODAY?**
7:00	**WHO CAN I MAKE SMILE TODAY?**
8:00	

EVENING PAGE

Day _____   *Date* _____

EVENING REFLECTIONS

MY BIG WINS TODAY

HOW DID I FEEL TODAY?

HOW DID I SHOW UP FOR THE PEOPLE IN MY LIFE TODAY?

HOW INTENTIONAL WAS I?

(1) (2) (3) (4) (5)

WATER? ☐   WORKOUT? ☐

WHAT GOT IN THE WAY?

1.

2.

3.

WHAT WILL I DO DIFFERENT?

MORNING PAGE

Day _____ *Date* _____

DAILY SCHEDULE	I AM GRATEFUL FOR...
6:00	
7:00	
8:00	
9:00	
10:00	**I AM STATEMENT ...**
11:00	**#1 GOAL TODAY**
12:00	
1:00	**TOP 5 PRIORITIES**
2:00	*1.*
3:00	*2.*
	3.
4:00	*4.*
5:00	*5.*
6:00	**WHO NEEDS ME AT 100% TODAY?**
7:00	**WHO CAN I MAKE SMILE TODAY?**
8:00	

EVENING PAGE

Day _____ *Date* _____

EVENING REFLECTIONS

MY BIG WINS TODAY

HOW DID I SHOW UP FOR THE PEOPLE IN MY LIFE TODAY?

HOW INTENTIONAL WAS I?

① ② ③ ④ ⑤

WATER? ☐   WORKOUT? ☐

WHAT GOT IN THE WAY?

1.

2.

3.

HOW DID I FEEL TODAY?

WHAT WILL I DO DIFFERENT?

MORNING PAGE

Day ———————— *Date* ————————

DAILY SCHEDULE	I AM GRATEFUL FOR...
6:00	
7:00	
8:00	
9:00	
10:00	**I AM STATEMENT ...**
11:00	
12:00	**#1 GOAL TODAY**
1:00	
2:00	**TOP 5 PRIORITIES**
3:00	*1.*
	2.
4:00	*3.*
	4.
5:00	*5.*
6:00	**WHO NEEDS ME AT 100% TODAY?**
7:00	
	WHO CAN I MAKE SMILE TODAY?
8:00	

EVENING PAGE

Day _____ *Date* _____

EVENING REFLECTIONS

MY BIG WINS TODAY

HOW DID I FEEL TODAY?

HOW DID I SHOW UP FOR THE PEOPLE IN MY LIFE TODAY?

HOW INTENTIONAL WAS I?

① ② ③ ④ ⑤

WATER? ☐   WORKOUT? ☐

WHAT GOT IN THE WAY?

1.
2.
3.

WHAT WILL I DO DIFFERENT?

MORNING PAGE

Day _____ *Date* _____

DAILY SCHEDULE	I AM GRATEFUL FOR...
6:00	⬡
7:00	⬡
8:00	⬡
9:00	
10:00	**I AM STATEMENT ...**
11:00	
12:00	**#1 GOAL TODAY**
1:00	**TOP 5 PRIORITIES**
2:00	*1.*
3:00	*2.*
	3.
4:00	*4.*
5:00	*5.*
6:00	**WHO NEEDS ME AT 100% TODAY?**
7:00	**WHO CAN I MAKE SMILE TODAY?**
8:00	

EVENING PAGE

Day _____ *Date* _____

EVENING REFLECTIONS

HOW DID I SHOW UP FOR THE PEOPLE IN MY LIFE TODAY?

MY BIG WINS TODAY

HOW INTENTIONAL WAS I?

(1) (2) (3) (4) (5)

WATER? ☐   WORKOUT? ☐

WHAT GOT IN THE WAY?

1.
2.
3.

HOW DID I FEEL TODAY?

WHAT WILL I DO DIFFERENT?

MORNING PAGE

Day ——————— *Date* ———————

DAILY SCHEDULE	I AM GRATEFUL FOR...
6:00	
7:00	
8:00	
9:00	
10:00	**I AM STATEMENT ...**
11:00	
12:00	**#1 GOAL TODAY**
1:00	
2:00	**TOP 5 PRIORITIES**
3:00	*1.*
	2.
4:00	*3.*
	4.
5:00	*5.*
6:00	**WHO NEEDS ME AT 100% TODAY?**
7:00	**WHO CAN I MAKE SMILE TODAY?**
8:00	

EVENING PAGE

Day _____ *Date* _____

EVENING REFLECTIONS	HOW DID I SHOW UP FOR THE PEOPLE IN MY LIFE TODAY?

MY BIG WINS TODAY

HOW INTENTIONAL WAS I?

① ② ③ ④ ⑤

WATER? ☐   WORKOUT? ☐

WHAT GOT IN THE WAY?

1.
2.
3.

HOW DID I FEEL TODAY?

WHAT WILL I DO DIFFERENT?

MORNING PAGE

Day _____ *Date* _____

DAILY SCHEDULE	I AM GRATEFUL FOR...
6:00	
7:00	
8:00	
9:00	
10:00	**I AM STATEMENT ...**
11:00	
12:00	**#1 GOAL TODAY**
1:00	
2:00	**TOP 5 PRIORITIES**
3:00	*1.*
4:00	*2.*
5:00	*3.*
	4.
6:00	*5.*
	WHO NEEDS ME AT 100% TODAY?
7:00	
	WHO CAN I MAKE SMILE TODAY?
8:00	

EVENING PAGE

Day —————————— *Date* ——————————

EVENING REFLECTIONS

HOW DID I SHOW UP FOR THE PEOPLE IN MY LIFE TODAY?

MY BIG WINS TODAY

HOW INTENTIONAL WAS I?

① ② ③ ④ ⑤

WATER? ☐   WORKOUT? ☐

WHAT GOT IN THE WAY?

1.

2.

3.

HOW DID I FEEL TODAY?

WHAT WILL I DO DIFFERENT?

Week Four

WEEKLY REVIEW

Month _____ *Date* _____

INSTRUCTIONS: On a scale of 1-5 (5 being the best-as in I did it every day, 4-almost every day, 3-half the time, 2-barely did what I needed, 1-fell off the wagon this week) how successful were you at your daily intentions for the following:

WORKOUTS: DID YOU MOVE AT LEAST 30 MIN DAILY?

NUTRITION: DID YOU EAT WELL BALANCED MEALS & TRACK EACH DAY(IF TRACKING)? DID YOU EAT TO FUEL FOR YOUR NEEDS & RESULTS YOU DESIRE?

HYDRATION: DID YOU DRINK ENOUGH WATER?
(½ BODY WEIGHT IN OZ PER DAY)

PRIORITIES & ACCOMPLISHMENT: DID YOU ACCOMPLISH EVERYTHING YOU INTENDED? (NOTE UNFINISHED BUSINESS BELOW)

SLEEP: DID YOU GET TO BED EACH NIGHT AND WAKE UP ON TIME? (WHAT DO YOU NEED TO DO DIFFERENTLY NEXT WEEK?

Week In Reflection

Yay! You showed up this week!! What were your biggest reflections, wins, memories, and challenges? How will you use this to fuel you forward into next week?

Week Five

SETTING INTENTIONS

Month _____ *Date* _____

PICK ONE GOAL TO FOCUS ON THIS WEEK:

MON	**I "GET TO" LIST**
TUES	
WED	
THURS	**NOTES**
FRI	
SAT	**SOCIAL INTENTIONS**
SUN	1. 2. 3.

Notes, Quotes, and Relfections

MORNING PAGE

Day _____ *Date* _____

DAILY SCHEDULE	I AM GRATEFUL FOR...
6:00	
7:00	
8:00	
9:00	
10:00	**I AM STATEMENT ...**
11:00	
12:00	**#1 GOAL TODAY**
1:00	
2:00	**TOP 5 PRIORITIES**
3:00	*1.*
4:00	*2.*
5:00	*3.*
6:00	*4.*
7:00	*5.*
8:00	**WHO NEEDS ME AT 100% TODAY?**

WHO CAN I MAKE SMILE TODAY?

EVENING PAGE

Day ———————— *Date* ————————

EVENING REFLECTIONS

HOW DID I SHOW UP FOR THE PEOPLE IN MY LIFE TODAY?

MY BIG WINS TODAY

HOW INTENTIONAL WAS I?

①　②　③　④　⑤

WATER? ☐　　WORKOUT? ☐

WHAT GOT IN THE WAY?

1.

2.

3.

HOW DID I FEEL TODAY?

WHAT WILL I DO DIFFERENT?

MORNING PAGE

Day ———————— *Date* ————————

DAILY SCHEDULE	I AM GRATEFUL FOR...
6:00	
7:00	
8:00	
9:00	
10:00	**I AM STATEMENT ...**
11:00	
12:00	**#1 GOAL TODAY**
1:00	
2:00	**TOP 5 PRIORITIES**
3:00	*1.*
	2.
4:00	*3.*
	4.
5:00	*5.*
6:00	**WHO NEEDS ME AT 100% TODAY?**
7:00	**WHO CAN I MAKE SMILE TODAY?**
8:00	

EVENING PAGE

Day ——————— *Date* ———————

EVENING REFLECTIONS	HOW DID I SHOW UP FOR THE PEOPLE IN MY LIFE TODAY?

MY BIG WINS TODAY

HOW INTENTIONAL WAS I?

① ② ③ ④ ⑤

WATER? ☐   WORKOUT? ☐

WHAT GOT IN THE WAY?

1.

2.

3.

HOW DID I FEEL TODAY?

WHAT WILL I DO DIFFERENT?

MORNING PAGE

Day _____ *Date* _____

DAILY SCHEDULE	I AM GRATEFUL FOR...
6:00	
7:00	
8:00	
9:00	
10:00	**I AM STATEMENT ...**
11:00	
12:00	**#1 GOAL TODAY**
1:00	
2:00	**TOP 5 PRIORITIES**
3:00	*1.*
4:00	*2.*
	3.
5:00	*4.*
	5.
6:00	**WHO NEEDS ME AT 100% TODAY?**
7:00	**WHO CAN I MAKE SMILE TODAY?**
8:00	

EVENING PAGE

Day _____ *Date* _____

EVENING REFLECTIONS	HOW DID I SHOW UP FOR THE PEOPLE IN MY LIFE TODAY?

MY BIG WINS TODAY

HOW INTENTIONAL WAS I?

① ② ③ ④ ⑤

WATER? ☐   WORKOUT? ☐

WHAT GOT IN THE WAY?

1.

2.

3.

HOW DID I FEEL TODAY?

WHAT WILL I DO DIFFERENT?

MORNING PAGE

Day ——————— *Date* ———————

DAILY SCHEDULE
6:00
7:00
8:00
9:00
10:00
11:00
12:00
1:00
2:00
3:00
4:00
5:00
6:00
7:00
8:00

I AM GRATEFUL FOR...

I AM STATEMENT ...

#1 GOAL TODAY

TOP 5 PRIORITIES

1.

2.

3.

4.

5.

WHO NEEDS ME AT 100% TODAY?

WHO CAN I MAKE SMILE TODAY?

EVENING PAGE

Day _____ *Date* _____

EVENING REFLECTIONS

HOW DID I SHOW UP FOR THE PEOPLE IN MY LIFE TODAY?

MY BIG WINS TODAY

HOW INTENTIONAL WAS I?

① ② ③ ④ ⑤

WATER? ☐　　WORKOUT? ☐

WHAT GOT IN THE WAY?

1.
2.
3.

HOW DID I FEEL TODAY?

WHAT WILL I DO DIFFERENT?

MORNING PAGE

Day ——————— *Date* ———————

DAILY SCHEDULE	I AM GRATEFUL FOR...
6:00	
7:00	
8:00	
9:00	

I AM STATEMENT ...

#1 GOAL TODAY

TOP 5 PRIORITIES

DAILY SCHEDULE (cont.)	
10:00	
11:00	
12:00	
1:00	
2:00	*1.*
3:00	*2.*
	3.
4:00	*4.*
5:00	*5.*
6:00	**WHO NEEDS ME AT 100% TODAY?**
7:00	**WHO CAN I MAKE SMILE TODAY?**
8:00	

EVENING PAGE

Day _____ *Date* _____

EVENING REFLECTIONS

MY BIG WINS TODAY

HOW DID I FEEL TODAY?

HOW DID I SHOW UP FOR THE PEOPLE IN MY LIFE TODAY?

HOW INTENTIONAL WAS I?

① ② ③ ④ ⑤

WATER? ☐   WORKOUT? ☐

WHAT GOT IN THE WAY?

1.

2.

3.

WHAT WILL I DO DIFFERENT?

MORNING PAGE

Day _____ *Date* _____

DAILY SCHEDULE	I AM GRATEFUL FOR...
6:00	
7:00	
8:00	
9:00	
10:00	**I AM STATEMENT ...**
11:00	
12:00	**#1 GOAL TODAY**
1:00	
2:00	**TOP 5 PRIORITIES**
3:00	*1.*
	2.
4:00	*3.*
	4.
5:00	*5.*
6:00	**WHO NEEDS ME AT 100% TODAY?**
7:00	**WHO CAN I MAKE SMILE TODAY?**
8:00	

EVENING PAGE

Day ———————— *Date* ————————

EVENING REFLECTIONS

HOW DID I SHOW UP FOR THE PEOPLE IN MY LIFE TODAY?

MY BIG WINS TODAY

HOW INTENTIONAL WAS I?

1 2 3 4 5

WATER? ☐   WORKOUT? ☐

WHAT GOT IN THE WAY?

1.

2.

3.

HOW DID I FEEL TODAY?

WHAT WILL I DO DIFFERENT?

MORNING PAGE

Day —————— *Date* ——————

DAILY SCHEDULE	I AM GRATEFUL FOR...
6:00	
7:00	
8:00	
9:00	
10:00	**I AM STATEMENT ...**
11:00	
12:00	**#1 GOAL TODAY**
1:00	
2:00	**TOP 5 PRIORITIES**
	1.
3:00	*2.*
	3.
4:00	*4.*
5:00	*5.*
6:00	**WHO NEEDS ME AT 100% TODAY?**
7:00	**WHO CAN I MAKE SMILE TODAY?**
8:00	

EVENING PAGE

Day —————— *Date* ——————

EVENING REFLECTIONS

HOW DID I SHOW UP FOR THE PEOPLE IN MY LIFE TODAY?

MY BIG WINS TODAY

HOW INTENTIONAL WAS I?

(1) (2) (3) (4) (5)

WATER? ☐   WORKOUT? ☐

WHAT GOT IN THE WAY?

1.

2.

3.

HOW DID I FEEL TODAY?

WHAT WILL I DO DIFFERENT?

Week Five

WEEKLY REVIEW

Month _____ *Date* _____

INSTRUCTIONS: On a scale of 1-5 (5 being the best-as in I did it every day, 4-almost every day, 3-half the time, 2-barely did what I needed, 1-fell off the wagon this week) how successful were you at your daily intentions for the following:

⬡ **WORKOUTS:** DID YOU MOVE AT LEAST 30 MIN DAILY?

⬡ **NUTRITION:** DID YOU EAT WELL BALANCED MEALS & TRACK EACH DAY(IF TRACKING)? DID YOU EAT TO FUEL FOR YOUR NEEDS & RESULTS YOU DESIRE?

⬡ **HYDRATION:** DID YOU DRINK ENOUGH WATER?
(½ BODY WEIGHT IN OZ PER DAY)

⬡ **PRIORITIES & ACCOMPLISHMENT:** DID YOU ACCOMPLISH EVERYTHING YOU INTENDED? (NOTE UNFINISHED BUSINESS BELOW)

⬡ **SLEEP:** DID YOU GET TO BED EACH NIGHT AND WAKE UP ON TIME? (WHAT DO YOU NEED TO DO DIFFERENTLY NEXT WEEK?

Week In Reflection

Yay! You showed up this week!! What were your biggest reflections, wins, memories, and challenges? How will you use this to fuel you forward into next week?

Monthly Review

THE FIRST MONTH

Month _____   *Date* _____

Instructions: Rate your life across all 8 pillars from 1-5.

- Health & Fitness
- Career
- Personal Growth
- Spirituality
- Relationships
- Social & Liesure
- Quality of Life
- Finances

CELEBRATING WINS

Share your favorite memories this month:

_____

_____

What are your big wins for this month?

_____

_____

How did you celebrate them?

_____

_____

OVERCOMING OBSTACLES

What "life situation" came up this month that may have derailed you?

_____

_____

How will you overcome it or manage the obstacle?

_____

_____

What would your future self tell you to do today to start momentum?

_____

_____

WHAT DO YOU WANT TO IMPROVE?

1.

2.

3.

HOW DO YOU FEEL IN YOUR BODY?

WHO HELD YOU ACCOUNTABLE?

Month

TWO

Monthly Intentions

THE SECOND MONTH

Month _____   *Date* _____

GOALS FOR THE MONTH

WHO/WHAT AM I GRATEFUL FOR?

THE "I GET TO" LIST

HOW WILL I SHOW UP THIS MONTH FOR MY PEOPLE?

Week One

SETTING INTENTIONS

Month —————— *Date* ——————

PICK ONE GOAL TO FOCUS ON THIS WEEK:

		I "GET TO" LIST
MON		
TUES		⬡
WED		⬡ ⬡ ⬡
THURS		**NOTES**
FRI		
SAT		**SOCIAL INTENTIONS**
SUN		*1.* *2.* *3.*

Notes, Quotes, and Relfections

MORNING PAGE

Day _____ *Date* _____

DAILY SCHEDULE

6:00

7:00

8:00

9:00

10:00

11:00

12:00

1:00

2:00

3:00

4:00

5:00

6:00

7:00

8:00

I AM GRATEFUL FOR...

I AM STATEMENT ...

#1 GOAL TODAY

TOP 5 PRIORITIES

1.

2.

3.

4.

5.

WHO NEEDS ME AT 100% TODAY?

WHO CAN I MAKE SMILE TODAY?

EVENING PAGE

Day _____ *Date* _____

EVENING REFLECTIONS

HOW DID I SHOW UP FOR THE PEOPLE IN MY LIFE TODAY?

MY BIG WINS TODAY

HOW INTENTIONAL WAS I?

(1) (2) (3) (4) (5)

WATER? ☐   WORKOUT? ☐

WHAT GOT IN THE WAY?

1.

2.

3.

HOW DID I FEEL TODAY?

WHAT WILL I DO DIFFERENT?

MORNING PAGE

Day _____ *Date* _____

DAILY SCHEDULE	I AM GRATEFUL FOR...
6:00	
7:00	
8:00	
9:00	
10:00	**I AM STATEMENT ...**
11:00	
12:00	**#1 GOAL TODAY**
1:00	
2:00	**TOP 5 PRIORITIES**
3:00	*1.*
4:00	*2.*
5:00	*3.*
	4.
	5.
6:00	**WHO NEEDS ME AT 100% TODAY?**
7:00	**WHO CAN I MAKE SMILE TODAY?**
8:00	

EVENING PAGE

Day _____ *Date* _____

EVENING REFLECTIONS

HOW DID I SHOW UP FOR THE PEOPLE IN MY LIFE TODAY?

MY BIG WINS TODAY

HOW INTENTIONAL WAS I?

① ② ③ ④ ⑤

WATER? ☐   WORKOUT? ☐

WHAT GOT IN THE WAY?

1. _____

2. _____

3. _____

HOW DID I FEEL TODAY?

WHAT WILL I DO DIFFERENT?

MORNING PAGE

Day _____ *Date* _____

DAILY SCHEDULE	I AM GRATEFUL FOR...
6:00	
7:00	
8:00	
9:00	

I AM STATEMENT ...

#1 GOAL TODAY

TOP 5 PRIORITIES

1.

2.

3.

4.

5.

WHO NEEDS ME AT 100% TODAY?

WHO CAN I MAKE SMILE TODAY?

Daily Schedule times:

- 6:00
- 7:00
- 8:00
- 9:00
- 10:00
- 11:00
- 12:00
- 1:00
- 2:00
- 3:00
- 4:00
- 5:00
- 6:00
- 7:00
- 8:00

EVENING PAGE

Day _____ *Date* _____

EVENING REFLECTIONS

HOW DID I SHOW UP FOR THE PEOPLE IN MY LIFE TODAY?

MY BIG WINS TODAY

HOW INTENTIONAL WAS I?

① ② ③ ④ ⑤

WATER? ☐   WORKOUT? ☐

WHAT GOT IN THE WAY?

1.
2.
3.

HOW DID I FEEL TODAY?

WHAT WILL I DO DIFFERENT?

MORNING PAGE

Day ———————— *Date* ————————

DAILY SCHEDULE	I AM GRATEFUL FOR...
6:00	
7:00	
8:00	
9:00	
10:00	**I AM STATEMENT ...**
11:00	
12:00	**#1 GOAL TODAY**
1:00	
2:00	**TOP 5 PRIORITIES**
	1.
3:00	*2.*
	3.
4:00	*4.*
5:00	*5.*
6:00	**WHO NEEDS ME AT 100% TODAY?**
7:00	**WHO CAN I MAKE SMILE TODAY?**
8:00	

EVENING PAGE

Day _____ *Date* _____

EVENING REFLECTIONS

HOW DID I SHOW UP FOR THE PEOPLE IN MY LIFE TODAY?

MY BIG WINS TODAY

HOW INTENTIONAL WAS I?

① ② ③ ④ ⑤

WATER? ☐   WORKOUT? ☐

WHAT GOT IN THE WAY?

1.
2.
3.

HOW DID I FEEL TODAY?

WHAT WILL I DO DIFFERENT?

MORNING PAGE

Day _____ *Date* _____

DAILY SCHEDULE

6:00

7:00

8:00

9:00

10:00

11:00

12:00

1:00

2:00

3:00

4:00

5:00

6:00

7:00

8:00

I AM GRATEFUL FOR...

I AM STATEMENT ...

#1 GOAL TODAY

TOP 5 PRIORITIES

1.

2.

3.

4.

5.

WHO NEEDS ME AT 100% TODAY?

WHO CAN I MAKE SMILE TODAY?

EVENING PAGE

Day _____ *Date* _____

EVENING REFLECTIONS

HOW DID I SHOW UP FOR THE PEOPLE IN MY LIFE TODAY?

MY BIG WINS TODAY

HOW INTENTIONAL WAS I?

① ② ③ ④ ⑤

WATER? ☐   WORKOUT? ☐

WHAT GOT IN THE WAY?

1.
2.
3.

HOW DID I FEEL TODAY?

WHAT WILL I DO DIFFERENT?

MORNING PAGE

Day ———————— *Date* ————————

DAILY SCHEDULE	I AM GRATEFUL FOR...
6:00	
7:00	
8:00	
9:00	
10:00	**I AM STATEMENT ...**
11:00	
12:00	**#1 GOAL TODAY**
1:00	
2:00	**TOP 5 PRIORITIES**
3:00	*1.*
	2.
4:00	*3.*
	4.
5:00	*5.*
6:00	**WHO NEEDS ME AT 100% TODAY?**
7:00	**WHO CAN I MAKE SMILE TODAY?**
8:00	

EVENING PAGE

Day _____ *Date* _____

EVENING REFLECTIONS

MY BIG WINS TODAY

HOW DID I SHOW UP FOR THE PEOPLE IN MY LIFE TODAY?

HOW INTENTIONAL WAS I?

(1) (2) (3) (4) (5)

WATER? ☐   WORKOUT? ☐

WHAT GOT IN THE WAY?

1.
2.
3.

HOW DID I FEEL TODAY?

WHAT WILL I DO DIFFERENT?

MORNING PAGE

Day _____ *Date* _____

DAILY SCHEDULE	I AM GRATEFUL FOR...
6:00	
7:00	
8:00	
9:00	
10:00	**I AM STATEMENT ...**
11:00	
12:00	**#1 GOAL TODAY**
1:00	
2:00	**TOP 5 PRIORITIES** *1.*
3:00	*2.*
4:00	*3.* *4.*
5:00	*5.*
6:00	**WHO NEEDS ME AT 100% TODAY?**
7:00	**WHO CAN I MAKE SMILE TODAY?**
8:00	

EVENING PAGE

Day _____ *Date* _____

EVENING REFLECTIONS

HOW DID I SHOW UP FOR THE PEOPLE IN MY LIFE TODAY?

MY BIG WINS TODAY

HOW INTENTIONAL WAS I?

① ② ③ ④ ⑤

WATER? ☐   WORKOUT? ☐

WHAT GOT IN THE WAY?

1.
2.
3.

HOW DID I FEEL TODAY?

WHAT WILL I DO DIFFERENT?

Week One

WEEKLY REVIEW

Month _____   *Date* _____

INSTRUCTIONS: On a scale of 1-5 (5 being the best-as in I did it every day, 4-almost every day, 3-half the time, 2-barely did what I needed, 1-fell off the wagon this week) how successful were you at your daily intentions for the following:

⬢ **WORKOUTS:** DID YOU MOVE AT LEAST 30 MIN DAILY?

⬢ **NUTRITION:** DID YOU EAT WELL BALANCED MEALS & TRACK EACH DAY(IF TRACKING)? DID YOU EAT TO FUEL FOR YOUR NEEDS & RESULTS YOU DESIRE?

⬢ **HYDRATION:** DID YOU DRINK ENOUGH WATER?
(½ BODY WEIGHT IN OZ PER DAY)

⬢ **PRIORITIES & ACCOMPLISHMENT:** DID YOU ACCOMPLISH EVERYTHING YOU INTENDED? (NOTE UNFINISHED BUSINESS BELOW)

⬢ **SLEEP:** DID YOU GET TO BED EACH NIGHT AND WAKE UP ON TIME? (WHAT DO YOU NEED TO DO DIFFERENTLY NEXT WEEK?

Week In Reflection

Yay! You showed up this week!! What were your biggest reflections, wins, memories, and challenges? How will you use this to fuel you forward into next week?

Week Two

SETTING INTENTIONS

Month _____ *Date* _____

PICK ONE GOAL TO FOCUS ON THIS WEEK:

MON	
TUES	
WED	
THURS	
FRI	
SAT	
SUN	

I "GET TO" LIST

NOTES

SOCIAL INTENTIONS

1.

2.

3.

Notes, Quotes, and Relfections

MORNING PAGE

Day _____ *Date* _____

DAILY SCHEDULE	I AM GRATEFUL FOR...
6:00	
7:00	
8:00	
9:00	
10:00	**I AM STATEMENT ...**
11:00	
12:00	**#1 GOAL TODAY**
1:00	
2:00	**TOP 5 PRIORITIES**
	1.
3:00	*2.*
	3.
4:00	*4.*
5:00	*5.*
6:00	**WHO NEEDS ME AT 100% TODAY?**
7:00	
	WHO CAN I MAKE SMILE TODAY?
8:00	

EVENING PAGE

Day _____ *Date* _____

EVENING REFLECTIONS

HOW DID I SHOW UP FOR THE PEOPLE IN MY LIFE TODAY?

MY BIG WINS TODAY

HOW INTENTIONAL WAS I?

① ② ③ ④ ⑤

WATER? ☐   WORKOUT? ☐

WHAT GOT IN THE WAY?

1.

2.

3.

HOW DID I FEEL TODAY?

WHAT WILL I DO DIFFERENT?

MORNING PAGE

Day _____ *Date* _____

DAILY SCHEDULE	I AM GRATEFUL FOR...
6:00	
7:00	
8:00	
9:00	
10:00	**I AM STATEMENT ...**
11:00	
12:00	**#1 GOAL TODAY**
1:00	
2:00	**TOP 5 PRIORITIES**
3:00	*1.*
	2.
	3.
4:00	*4.*
5:00	*5.*
6:00	**WHO NEEDS ME AT 100% TODAY?**
7:00	
8:00	**WHO CAN I MAKE SMILE TODAY?**

EVENING PAGE

Day _____ *Date* _____

EVENING REFLECTIONS

HOW DID I SHOW UP FOR THE PEOPLE IN MY LIFE TODAY?

MY BIG WINS TODAY

HOW INTENTIONAL WAS I?

(1) (2) (3) (4) (5)

WATER? ☐   WORKOUT? ☐

WHAT GOT IN THE WAY?

1.

2.

3.

HOW DID I FEEL TODAY?

WHAT WILL I DO DIFFERENT?

MORNING PAGE

Day _____ *Date* _____

DAILY SCHEDULE	I AM GRATEFUL FOR...
6:00	
7:00	
8:00	
9:00	
10:00	**I AM STATEMENT ...**
11:00	
12:00	**#1 GOAL TODAY**
1:00	
2:00	**TOP 5 PRIORITIES**
3:00	*1.*
	2.
4:00	*3.*
	4.
5:00	*5.*
6:00	**WHO NEEDS ME AT 100% TODAY?**
7:00	**WHO CAN I MAKE SMILE TODAY?**
8:00	

EVENING PAGE

Day _____ Date _____

EVENING REFLECTIONS

HOW DID I SHOW UP FOR THE PEOPLE IN MY LIFE TODAY?

MY BIG WINS TODAY

HOW INTENTIONAL WAS I?

① ② ③ ④ ⑤

WATER? ☐   WORKOUT? ☐

WHAT GOT IN THE WAY?

1.
2.
3.

HOW DID I FEEL TODAY?

WHAT WILL I DO DIFFERENT?

MORNING PAGE

Day _____ *Date* _____

DAILY SCHEDULE	I AM GRATEFUL FOR...
6:00	
7:00	
8:00	
9:00	
10:00	**I AM STATEMENT ...**
11:00	
12:00	**#1 GOAL TODAY**
1:00	
2:00	**TOP 5 PRIORITIES**
3:00	*1.*
	2.
4:00	*3.*
	4.
5:00	*5.*
6:00	**WHO NEEDS ME AT 100% TODAY?**
7:00	
	WHO CAN I MAKE SMILE TODAY?
8:00	

EVENING PAGE

Day _____ *Date* _____

EVENING REFLECTIONS

MY BIG WINS TODAY

HOW DID I FEEL TODAY?

HOW DID I SHOW UP FOR THE PEOPLE IN MY LIFE TODAY?

HOW INTENTIONAL WAS I?

(1) (2) (3) (4) (5)

WATER? ☐   WORKOUT? ☐

WHAT GOT IN THE WAY?

1. _____
2. _____
3. _____

WHAT WILL I DO DIFFERENT?

MORNING PAGE

Day _____ *Date* _____

DAILY SCHEDULE	I AM GRATEFUL FOR...
6:00	
7:00	
8:00	
9:00	
10:00	**I AM STATEMENT ...**
11:00	**#1 GOAL TODAY**
12:00	
1:00	**TOP 5 PRIORITIES**
2:00	*1.*
3:00	*2.*
	3.
4:00	*4.*
5:00	*5.*
6:00	**WHO NEEDS ME AT 100% TODAY?**
7:00	**WHO CAN I MAKE SMILE TODAY?**
8:00	

EVENING PAGE

Day _____ *Date* _____

EVENING REFLECTIONS

HOW DID I SHOW UP FOR THE PEOPLE IN MY LIFE TODAY?

MY BIG WINS TODAY

HOW INTENTIONAL WAS I?

① ② ③ ④ ⑤

WATER? ☐   WORKOUT? ☐

WHAT GOT IN THE WAY?

1.
2.
3.

HOW DID I FEEL TODAY?

WHAT WILL I DO DIFFERENT?

MORNING PAGE

Day _____ *Date* _____

DAILY SCHEDULE	I AM GRATEFUL FOR...
6:00	
7:00	
8:00	
9:00	
10:00	**I AM STATEMENT ...**
11:00	**#1 GOAL TODAY**
12:00	
1:00	**TOP 5 PRIORITIES**
2:00	1.
3:00	2.
4:00	3.
5:00	4.
6:00	5.
7:00	**WHO NEEDS ME AT 100% TODAY?**
8:00	**WHO CAN I MAKE SMILE TODAY?**

EVENING PAGE

Day _____ *Date* _____

EVENING REFLECTIONS

HOW DID I SHOW UP FOR THE PEOPLE IN MY LIFE TODAY?

MY BIG WINS TODAY

HOW INTENTIONAL WAS I?

① ② ③ ④ ⑤

WATER? ☐   WORKOUT? ☐

WHAT GOT IN THE WAY?

1.

2.

3.

HOW DID I FEEL TODAY?

WHAT WILL I DO DIFFERENT?

MORNING PAGE

Day _____ *Date* _____

DAILY SCHEDULE	I AM GRATEFUL FOR...
6:00	
7:00	
8:00	
9:00	
10:00	**I AM STATEMENT ...**
11:00	
12:00	**#1 GOAL TODAY**
1:00	
2:00	**TOP 5 PRIORITIES** *1.*
3:00	*2.*
	3.
4:00	*4.*
5:00	*5.*
6:00	**WHO NEEDS ME AT 100% TODAY?**
7:00	**WHO CAN I MAKE SMILE TODAY?**
8:00	

EVENING PAGE

Day _____ *Date* _____

EVENING REFLECTIONS

HOW DID I SHOW UP FOR THE PEOPLE IN MY LIFE TODAY?

MY BIG WINS TODAY

HOW INTENTIONAL WAS I?

① ② ③ ④ ⑤

WATER? ☐   WORKOUT? ☐

WHAT GOT IN THE WAY?

1.

2.

3.

HOW DID I FEEL TODAY?

WHAT WILL I DO DIFFERENT?

Week Two

WEEKLY REVIEW

INSTRUCTIONS: On a scale of 1-5 (5 being the best-as in I did it every day, 4-almost every day, 3-half the time, 2-barely did what I needed, 1-fell off the wagon this week) how successful were you at your daily intentions for the following:

WORKOUTS: DID YOU MOVE AT LEAST 30 MIN DAILY?

NUTRITION: DID YOU EAT WELL BALANCED MEALS & TRACK EACH DAY(IF TRACKING)? DID YOU EAT TO FUEL FOR YOUR NEEDS & RESULTS YOU DESIRE?

HYDRATION: DID YOU DRINK ENOUGH WATER?
(½ BODY WEIGHT IN OZ PER DAY)

PRIORITIES & ACCOMPLISHMENT: DID YOU ACCOMPLISH EVERYTHING YOU INTENDED? (NOTE UNFINISHED BUSINESS BELOW)

SLEEP: DID YOU GET TO BED EACH NIGHT AND WAKE UP ON TIME? (WHAT DO YOU NEED TO DO DIFFERENTLY NEXT WEEK?

Week In Reflection

Yay! You showed up this week!! What were your biggest reflections, wins, memories, and challenges? How will you use this to fuel you forward into next week?

Week Three

SETTING INTENTIONS

Month _____ *Date* _____

"Crews Beyond Limits is not a fad, it's a lifestyle." -Krystalore Crews

PICK ONE GOAL TO FOCUS ON THIS WEEK:

MON	
TUES	
WED	
THURS	
FRI	
SAT	
SUN	

I "GET TO" LIST

NOTES

SOCIAL INTENTIONS

1.

2.

3.

Notes, Quotes, and Relfections

MORNING PAGE

*Day*_____ *Date*_____

DAILY SCHEDULE	I AM GRATEFUL FOR...
6:00	
7:00	
8:00	
9:00	**I AM STATEMENT ...**
10:00	
11:00	**#1 GOAL TODAY**
12:00	
1:00	**TOP 5 PRIORITIES**
2:00	*1.*
3:00	*2.*
4:00	*3.*
	4.
5:00	*5.*
6:00	**WHO NEEDS ME AT 100% TODAY?**
7:00	
	WHO CAN I MAKE SMILE TODAY?
8:00	

EVENING PAGE

EVENING REFLECTIONS

HOW DID I SHOW UP FOR THE PEOPLE IN MY LIFE TODAY?

MY BIG WINS TODAY

HOW INTENTIONAL WAS I?

① ② ③ ④ ⑤

WATER? ☐　　WORKOUT? ☐

WHAT GOT IN THE WAY?

1.

2.

3.

HOW DID I FEEL TODAY?

WHAT WILL I DO DIFFERENT?

MORNING PAGE

Day _____ *Date* _____

DAILY SCHEDULE	I AM GRATEFUL FOR...
6:00	
7:00	
8:00	
9:00	
10:00	**I AM STATEMENT ...**
11:00	
12:00	**#1 GOAL TODAY**
1:00	
2:00	**TOP 5 PRIORITIES**
3:00	*1.*
	2.
4:00	*3.*
	4.
5:00	*5.*
6:00	**WHO NEEDS ME AT 100% TODAY?**
7:00	
	WHO CAN I MAKE SMILE TODAY?
8:00	

EVENING PAGE

Day _____ *Date* _____

EVENING REFLECTIONS

MY BIG WINS TODAY

HOW DID I FEEL TODAY?

HOW DID I SHOW UP FOR THE PEOPLE IN MY LIFE TODAY?

HOW INTENTIONAL WAS I?

① ② ③ ④ ⑤

WATER? ☐   WORKOUT? ☐

WHAT GOT IN THE WAY?

1. _____
2. _____
3. _____

WHAT WILL I DO DIFFERENT?

MORNING PAGE

DAILY SCHEDULE

6:00

7:00

8:00

9:00

10:00

11:00

12:00

1:00

2:00

3:00

4:00

5:00

6:00

7:00

8:00

I AM GRATEFUL FOR...

I AM STATEMENT ...

#1 GOAL TODAY

TOP 5 PRIORITIES

1.

2.

3.

4.

5.

WHO NEEDS ME AT 100% TODAY?

WHO CAN I MAKE SMILE TODAY?

EVENING PAGE

Day _____ *Date* _____

EVENING REFLECTIONS

HOW DID I SHOW UP FOR THE PEOPLE IN MY LIFE TODAY?

MY BIG WINS TODAY

HOW INTENTIONAL WAS I?

1   2   3   4   5

WATER? ☐   WORKOUT? ☐

WHAT GOT IN THE WAY?

1.
2.
3.

HOW DID I FEEL TODAY?

WHAT WILL I DO DIFFERENT?

MORNING PAGE

Day _____ *Date* _____

DAILY SCHEDULE	I AM GRATEFUL FOR...
6:00	
7:00	
8:00	
9:00	
10:00	**I AM STATEMENT ...**
11:00	**#1 GOAL TODAY**
12:00	
1:00	**TOP 5 PRIORITIES**
2:00	*1.*
3:00	*2.*
	3.
4:00	*4.*
5:00	*5.*
6:00	**WHO NEEDS ME AT 100% TODAY?**
7:00	**WHO CAN I MAKE SMILE TODAY?**
8:00	

EVENING PAGE

Day —————————— *Date* ——————————

EVENING REFLECTIONS

MY BIG WINS TODAY

HOW DID I FEEL TODAY?

HOW DID I SHOW UP FOR THE PEOPLE IN MY LIFE TODAY?

HOW INTENTIONAL WAS I?

① ② ③ ④ ⑤

WATER? ☐   WORKOUT? ☐

WHAT GOT IN THE WAY?

1.

2.

3.

WHAT WILL I DO DIFFERENT?

MORNING PAGE

Day _____ *Date* _____

DAILY SCHEDULE	I AM GRATEFUL FOR...
6:00	
7:00	
8:00	
9:00	
10:00	**I AM STATEMENT ...**
11:00	**#1 GOAL TODAY**
12:00	
1:00	**TOP 5 PRIORITIES**
2:00	*1.*
3:00	*2.*
	3.
4:00	*4.*
5:00	*5.*
6:00	**WHO NEEDS ME AT 100% TODAY?**
7:00	**WHO CAN I MAKE SMILE TODAY?**
8:00	

EVENING PAGE

EVENING REFLECTIONS

MY BIG WINS TODAY

HOW DID I FEEL TODAY?

HOW DID I SHOW UP FOR THE PEOPLE IN MY LIFE TODAY?

HOW INTENTIONAL WAS I?

1 2 3 4 5

WATER? ☐   WORKOUT? ☐

WHAT GOT IN THE WAY?

1.
2.
3.

WHAT WILL I DO DIFFERENT?

MORNING PAGE

Day _____ *Date* _____

DAILY SCHEDULE

6:00

7:00

8:00

9:00

10:00

11:00

12:00

1:00

2:00

3:00

4:00

5:00

6:00

7:00

8:00

I AM GRATEFUL FOR...

I AM STATEMENT ...

#1 GOAL TODAY

TOP 5 PRIORITIES

1.

2.

3.

4.

5.

WHO NEEDS ME AT 100% TODAY?

WHO CAN I MAKE SMILE TODAY?

EVENING PAGE

Day _____ Date _____

EVENING REFLECTIONS

HOW DID I SHOW UP FOR THE PEOPLE IN MY LIFE TODAY?

MY BIG WINS TODAY

HOW INTENTIONAL WAS I?

① ② ③ ④ ⑤

WATER? ☐   WORKOUT? ☐

WHAT GOT IN THE WAY?

1.

2.

3.

HOW DID I FEEL TODAY?

WHAT WILL I DO DIFFERENT?

MORNING PAGE

Day _____ *Date* _____

DAILY SCHEDULE	I AM GRATEFUL FOR...
6:00	
7:00	
8:00	
9:00	
10:00	**I AM STATEMENT ...**
11:00	**#1 GOAL TODAY**
12:00	
1:00	**TOP 5 PRIORITIES**
2:00	*1.*
3:00	*2.*
4:00	*3.*
	4.
5:00	*5.*
6:00	**WHO NEEDS ME AT 100% TODAY?**
7:00	**WHO CAN I MAKE SMILE TODAY?**
8:00	

EVENING PAGE

Day _____ *Date* _____

EVENING REFLECTIONS

MY BIG WINS TODAY

HOW DID I FEEL TODAY?

HOW DID I SHOW UP FOR THE PEOPLE IN MY LIFE TODAY?

HOW INTENTIONAL WAS I?

(1) (2) (3) (4) (5)

WATER? ☐   WORKOUT? ☐

WHAT GOT IN THE WAY?

1.

2.

3.

WHAT WILL I DO DIFFERENT?

Week Three

WEEKLY REVIEW

Month ——————— *Date* ———————

INSTRUCTIONS: On a scale of 1-5 (5 being the best-as in I did it every day, 4-almost every day, 3-half the time, 2-barely did what I needed, 1-fell off the wagon this week) how successful were you at your daily intentions for the following:

⬡ **WORKOUTS:** DID YOU MOVE AT LEAST 30 MIN DAILY?

⬡ **NUTRITION:** DID YOU EAT WELL BALANCED MEALS & TRACK EACH DAY(IF TRACKING)? DID YOU EAT TO FUEL FOR YOUR NEEDS & RESULTS YOU DESIRE?

⬡ **HYDRATION:** DID YOU DRINK ENOUGH WATER?
(½ BODY WEIGHT IN OZ PER DAY)

⬡ **PRIORITIES & ACCOMPLISHMENT:** DID YOU ACCOMPLISH EVERYTHING YOU INTENDED? (NOTE UNFINISHED BUSINESS BELOW)

⬡ **SLEEP:** DID YOU GET TO BED EACH NIGHT AND WAKE UP ON TIME? (WHAT DO YOU NEED TO DO DIFFERENTLY NEXT WEEK?

Week In Reflection

Yay! You showed up this week!! What were your biggest reflections, wins, memories, and challenges? How will you use this to fuel you forward into next week?

Week Four

SETTING INTENTIONS

Month _____ *Date* _____

PICK ONE GOAL TO FOCUS ON THIS WEEK:

MON	**I "GET TO" LIST**
TUES	⬡ ⬡ ⬡ ⬡
WED	
THURS	**NOTES**
FRI	
SAT	**SOCIAL INTENTIONS**
SUN	1. 2. 3.

Notes, Quotes, and Relfections

MORNING PAGE

Day _____ *Date* _____

DAILY SCHEDULE	I AM GRATEFUL FOR...
6:00	
7:00	
8:00	
9:00	
10:00	**I AM STATEMENT ...**
11:00	**#1 GOAL TODAY**
12:00	
1:00	**TOP 5 PRIORITIES**
2:00	1.
3:00	2.
4:00	3.
	4.
5:00	5.
6:00	**WHO NEEDS ME AT 100% TODAY?**
7:00	**WHO CAN I MAKE SMILE TODAY?**
8:00	

EVENING PAGE

Day _____ *Date* _____

EVENING REFLECTIONS

HOW DID I SHOW UP FOR THE PEOPLE IN MY LIFE TODAY?

MY BIG WINS TODAY

HOW INTENTIONAL WAS I?

① ② ③ ④ ⑤

WATER? ☐   WORKOUT? ☐

WHAT GOT IN THE WAY?

1. _____
2. _____
3. _____

HOW DID I FEEL TODAY?

WHAT WILL I DO DIFFERENT?

MORNING PAGE

Day _____ Date _____

DAILY SCHEDULE	I AM GRATEFUL FOR...
6:00	
7:00	
8:00	
9:00	
10:00	**I AM STATEMENT ...**
11:00	
12:00	**#1 GOAL TODAY**
1:00	
2:00	**TOP 5 PRIORITIES**
3:00	*1.*
	2.
4:00	*3.*
	4.
5:00	*5.*
6:00	**WHO NEEDS ME AT 100% TODAY?**
7:00	**WHO CAN I MAKE SMILE TODAY?**
8:00	

EVENING PAGE

Day _____ *Date* _____

EVENING REFLECTIONS

HOW DID I SHOW UP FOR THE PEOPLE IN MY LIFE TODAY?

MY BIG WINS TODAY

HOW INTENTIONAL WAS I?

(1) (2) (3) (4) (5)

WATER? ☐   WORKOUT? ☐

WHAT GOT IN THE WAY?

1.

2.

3.

HOW DID I FEEL TODAY?

WHAT WILL I DO DIFFERENT?

MORNING PAGE

Day _____ *Date* _____

DAILY SCHEDULE	I AM GRATEFUL FOR...
6:00	
7:00	
8:00	
9:00	
10:00	**I AM STATEMENT ...**
11:00	**#1 GOAL TODAY**
12:00	
1:00	**TOP 5 PRIORITIES**
2:00	*1.*
3:00	*2.*
	3.
4:00	*4.*
5:00	*5.*
6:00	**WHO NEEDS ME AT 100% TODAY?**
7:00	**WHO CAN I MAKE SMILE TODAY?**
8:00	

EVENING PAGE

Day _____ *Date* _____

EVENING REFLECTIONS

HOW DID I SHOW UP FOR THE PEOPLE IN MY LIFE TODAY?

MY BIG WINS TODAY

HOW INTENTIONAL WAS I?

① ② ③ ④ ⑤

WATER? ☐   WORKOUT? ☐

WHAT GOT IN THE WAY?

1.

2.

3.

HOW DID I FEEL TODAY?

WHAT WILL I DO DIFFERENT?

MORNING PAGE

Day _____ *Date* _____

DAILY SCHEDULE	I AM GRATEFUL FOR...
6:00	
7:00	
8:00	
9:00	
10:00	**I AM STATEMENT ...**
11:00	
12:00	**#1 GOAL TODAY**
1:00	
2:00	**TOP 5 PRIORITIES**
3:00	*1.*
4:00	*2.*
	3.
5:00	*4.*
	5.
6:00	**WHO NEEDS ME AT 100% TODAY?**
7:00	
	WHO CAN I MAKE SMILE TODAY?
8:00	

EVENING PAGE

Day _____ *Date* _____

EVENING REFLECTIONS

HOW DID I SHOW UP FOR THE PEOPLE IN MY LIFE TODAY?

MY BIG WINS TODAY

HOW INTENTIONAL WAS I?

① ② ③ ④ ⑤

WATER? ☐   WORKOUT? ☐

WHAT GOT IN THE WAY?

1.

2.

3.

HOW DID I FEEL TODAY?

WHAT WILL I DO DIFFERENT?

MORNING PAGE

Day _____ *Date* _____

DAILY SCHEDULE	I AM GRATEFUL FOR...
6:00	
7:00	
8:00	
9:00	
10:00	**I AM STATEMENT ...**
11:00	**#1 GOAL TODAY**
12:00	
1:00	**TOP 5 PRIORITIES**
2:00	*1.*
3:00	*2.*
	3.
4:00	*4.*
5:00	*5.*
6:00	**WHO NEEDS ME AT 100% TODAY?**
7:00	
	WHO CAN I MAKE SMILE TODAY?
8:00	

EVENING PAGE

Day _____ *Date* _____

EVENING REFLECTIONS

HOW DID I SHOW UP FOR THE PEOPLE IN MY LIFE TODAY?

MY BIG WINS TODAY

HOW INTENTIONAL WAS I?

① ② ③ ④ ⑤

WATER? ☐   WORKOUT? ☐

WHAT GOT IN THE WAY?

1.

2.

3.

HOW DID I FEEL TODAY?

WHAT WILL I DO DIFFERENT?

MORNING PAGE

Day _____ *Date* _____

DAILY SCHEDULE	I AM GRATEFUL FOR...
6:00	
7:00	
8:00	
9:00	
10:00	**I AM STATEMENT ...**
11:00	
12:00	**#1 GOAL TODAY**
1:00	
2:00	**TOP 5 PRIORITIES**
3:00	*1.*
	2.
4:00	*3.*
	4.
5:00	*5.*
6:00	**WHO NEEDS ME AT 100% TODAY?**
7:00	**WHO CAN I MAKE SMILE TODAY?**
8:00	

EVENING PAGE

Day _____ *Date* _____

EVENING REFLECTIONS

HOW DID I SHOW UP FOR THE PEOPLE IN MY LIFE TODAY?

MY BIG WINS TODAY

HOW INTENTIONAL WAS I?

1   2   3   4   5

WATER? ☐   WORKOUT? ☐

WHAT GOT IN THE WAY?

1.

2.

3.

HOW DID I FEEL TODAY?

WHAT WILL I DO DIFFERENT?

MORNING PAGE

Day _____ *Date* _____

DAILY SCHEDULE	I AM GRATEFUL FOR...
6:00	
7:00	
8:00	
9:00	
10:00	**I AM STATEMENT ...**
11:00	
12:00	**#1 GOAL TODAY**
1:00	
2:00	**TOP 5 PRIORITIES**
3:00	*1.*
	2.
4:00	*3.*
	4.
5:00	*5.*
6:00	**WHO NEEDS ME AT 100% TODAY?**
7:00	**WHO CAN I MAKE SMILE TODAY?**
8:00	

EVENING PAGE

Day _____ *Date* _____

EVENING REFLECTIONS

MY BIG WINS TODAY

HOW DID I FEEL TODAY?

HOW DID I SHOW UP FOR THE PEOPLE IN MY LIFE TODAY?

HOW INTENTIONAL WAS I?

① ② ③ ④ ⑤

WATER? ☐   WORKOUT? ☐

WHAT GOT IN THE WAY?

1. _____
2. _____
3. _____

WHAT WILL I DO DIFFERENT?

Week Four

WEEKLY REVIEW

INSTRUCTIONS: On a scale of 1-5 (5 being the best-as in I did it every day, 4-almost every day, 3-half the time, 2-barely did what I needed, 1-fell off the wagon this week) how successful were you at your daily intentions for the following:

WORKOUTS: DID YOU MOVE AT LEAST 30 MIN DAILY?

NUTRITION: DID YOU EAT WELL BALANCED MEALS & TRACK EACH DAY(IF TRACKING)? DID YOU EAT TO FUEL FOR YOUR NEEDS & RESULTS YOU DESIRE?

HYDRATION: DID YOU DRINK ENOUGH WATER?
(½ BODY WEIGHT IN OZ PER DAY)

PRIORITIES & ACCOMPLISHMENT: DID YOU ACCOMPLISH EVERYTHING YOU INTENDED? (NOTE UNFINISHED BUSINESS BELOW)

SLEEP: DID YOU GET TO BED EACH NIGHT AND WAKE UP ON TIME? (WHAT DO YOU NEED TO DO DIFFERENTLY NEXT WEEK?

Week In Reflection

Yay! You showed up this week!! What were your biggest reflections, wins, memories, and challenges? How will you use this to fuel you forward into next week?

Week Five

SETTING INTENTIONS

Month ————— *Date* —————

PICK ONE GOAL TO FOCUS ON THIS WEEK:

MON	
TUES	**I "GET TO" LIST**
WED	
THURS	**NOTES**
FRI	
SAT	**SOCIAL INTENTIONS**
SUN	1. 2. 3.

Notes, Quotes, and Relfections

MORNING PAGE

Day _____ *Date* _____

DAILY SCHEDULE	I AM GRATEFUL FOR...
6:00	
7:00	
8:00	
9:00	
10:00	**I AM STATEMENT ...**
11:00	**#1 GOAL TODAY**
12:00	
1:00	**TOP 5 PRIORITIES**
2:00	*1.*
3:00	*2.*
4:00	*3.*
	4.
5:00	*5.*
6:00	**WHO NEEDS ME AT 100% TODAY?**
7:00	**WHO CAN I MAKE SMILE TODAY?**
8:00	

EVENING PAGE

Day _____ *Date* _____

EVENING REFLECTIONS

HOW DID I SHOW UP FOR THE PEOPLE IN MY LIFE TODAY?

MY BIG WINS TODAY

HOW INTENTIONAL WAS I?

① ② ③ ④ ⑤

WATER? ☐ WORKOUT? ☐

WHAT GOT IN THE WAY?

1.

2.

3.

HOW DID I FEEL TODAY?

WHAT WILL I DO DIFFERENT?

MORNING PAGE

Day _____ *Date* _____

DAILY SCHEDULE	I AM GRATEFUL FOR...
6:00	
7:00	
8:00	
9:00	
10:00	**I AM STATEMENT ...**
11:00	
12:00	**#1 GOAL TODAY**
1:00	
2:00	**TOP 5 PRIORITIES**
3:00	*1.*
	2.
4:00	*3.*
	4.
5:00	*5.*
6:00	**WHO NEEDS ME AT 100% TODAY?**
7:00	**WHO CAN I MAKE SMILE TODAY?**
8:00	

EVENING PAGE

Day _____ *Date* _____

EVENING REFLECTIONS

HOW DID I SHOW UP FOR THE PEOPLE IN MY LIFE TODAY?

MY BIG WINS TODAY

HOW INTENTIONAL WAS I?

① ② ③ ④ ⑤

WATER? ☐   WORKOUT? ☐

WHAT GOT IN THE WAY?

1.

2.

3.

HOW DID I FEEL TODAY?

WHAT WILL I DO DIFFERENT?

MORNING PAGE

Day _____ *Date* _____

DAILY SCHEDULE	I AM GRATEFUL FOR...
6:00	
7:00	
8:00	
9:00	
10:00	**I AM STATEMENT ...**
11:00	
12:00	**#1 GOAL TODAY**
1:00	
2:00	**TOP 5 PRIORITIES**
3:00	*1.*
4:00	*2.*
5:00	*3.*
	4.
	5.
6:00	**WHO NEEDS ME AT 100% TODAY?**
7:00	**WHO CAN I MAKE SMILE TODAY?**
8:00	

EVENING PAGE

Day _____ Date _____

EVENING REFLECTIONS

HOW DID I SHOW UP FOR THE PEOPLE IN MY LIFE TODAY?

MY BIG WINS TODAY

HOW INTENTIONAL WAS I?

1 2 3 4 5

WATER? ☐   WORKOUT? ☐

WHAT GOT IN THE WAY?

1.

2.

3.

HOW DID I FEEL TODAY?

WHAT WILL I DO DIFFERENT?

MORNING PAGE

Day _____ *Date* _____

DAILY SCHEDULE	I AM GRATEFUL FOR...
6:00	
7:00	
8:00	
9:00	
	I AM STATEMENT ...
10:00	
11:00	**#1 GOAL TODAY**
12:00	
1:00	**TOP 5 PRIORITIES**
2:00	*1.*
3:00	*2.*
	3.
4:00	*4.*
5:00	*5.*
6:00	**WHO NEEDS ME AT 100% TODAY?**
7:00	**WHO CAN I MAKE SMILE TODAY?**
8:00	

EVENING PAGE

Day _____ *Date* _____

EVENING REFLECTIONS

HOW DID I SHOW UP FOR THE PEOPLE IN MY LIFE TODAY?

MY BIG WINS TODAY

HOW INTENTIONAL WAS I?

(1) (2) (3) (4) (5)

WATER? ☐   WORKOUT? ☐

WHAT GOT IN THE WAY?

1.
2.
3.

HOW DID I FEEL TODAY?

WHAT WILL I DO DIFFERENT?

MORNING PAGE

Day _____ *Date* _____

DAILY SCHEDULE	I AM GRATEFUL FOR...
6:00	
7:00	
8:00	
9:00	
10:00	**I AM STATEMENT ...**
11:00	**#1 GOAL TODAY**
12:00	
1:00	**TOP 5 PRIORITIES**
2:00	*1.*
3:00	*2.*
4:00	*3.*
	4.
5:00	*5.*
6:00	**WHO NEEDS ME AT 100% TODAY?**
7:00	**WHO CAN I MAKE SMILE TODAY?**
8:00	

EVENING PAGE

Day _____ *Date* _____

EVENING REFLECTIONS

MY BIG WINS TODAY

HOW DID I SHOW UP FOR THE PEOPLE IN MY LIFE TODAY?

HOW INTENTIONAL WAS I?

① ② ③ ④ ⑤

WATER? ☐   WORKOUT? ☐

WHAT GOT IN THE WAY?

1.

2.

3.

HOW DID I FEEL TODAY?

WHAT WILL I DO DIFFERENT?

MORNING PAGE

Day _____ *Date* _____

DAILY SCHEDULE	I AM GRATEFUL FOR...

DAILY SCHEDULE

6:00

7:00

8:00

9:00

10:00

11:00

12:00

1:00

2:00

3:00

4:00

5:00

6:00

7:00

8:00

I AM GRATEFUL FOR...

I AM STATEMENT ...

#1 GOAL TODAY

TOP 5 PRIORITIES

1.

2.

3.

4.

5.

WHO NEEDS ME AT 100% TODAY?

WHO CAN I MAKE SMILE TODAY?

EVENING PAGE

Day _____ *Date* _____

EVENING REFLECTIONS

HOW DID I SHOW UP FOR THE PEOPLE IN MY LIFE TODAY?

MY BIG WINS TODAY

HOW INTENTIONAL WAS I?

① ② ③ ④ ⑤

WATER? ☐   WORKOUT? ☐

WHAT GOT IN THE WAY?

1.
2.
3.

HOW DID I FEEL TODAY?

WHAT WILL I DO DIFFERENT?

Week Five

WEEKLY REVIEW

Month _____ *Date* _____

INSTRUCTIONS: On a scale of 1-5 (5 being the best-as in I did it every day, 4-almost every day, 3-half the time, 2-barely did what I needed, 1-fell off the wagon this week) how successful were you at your daily intentions for the following:

WORKOUTS: DID YOU MOVE AT LEAST 30 MIN DAILY?

NUTRITION: DID YOU EAT WELL BALANCED MEALS & TRACK EACH DAY(IF TRACKING)? DID YOU EAT TO FUEL FOR YOUR NEEDS & RESULTS YOU DESIRE?

HYDRATION: DID YOU DRINK ENOUGH WATER?
(½ BODY WEIGHT IN OZ PER DAY)

PRIORITIES & ACCOMPLISHMENT: DID YOU ACCOMPLISH EVERYTHING YOU INTENDED? (NOTE UNFINISHED BUSINESS BELOW)

SLEEP: DID YOU GET TO BED EACH NIGHT AND WAKE UP ON TIME? (WHAT DO YOU NEED TO DO DIFFERENTLY NEXT WEEK?

Week In Reflection

Yay! You showed up this week!! What were your biggest reflections, wins, memories, and challenges? How will you use this to fuel you forward into next week?

Monthly Review

THE SECOND MONTH

Month _____ *Date* _____

Instructions: Rate your life across all 8 pillars from 1-5.

⬡ Health & Fitness   ⬡ Career   ⬡ Personal Growth   ⬡ Spirituality

⬡ Relationships   ⬡ Social & Liesure   ⬡ Quality of Life   ⬡ Finances

---

CELEBRATING WINS

Share your favorite memories this month:

_____

_____

What are your big wins for this month?

_____

_____

How did you celebrate them?

_____

_____

OVERCOMING OBSTACLES

What "life situation" came up this month that may have derailed you?

_____

_____

How will you overcome it or manage the obstacle?

_____

_____

What would your future self tell you to do today to start momentum?

_____

_____

WHAT DO YOU WANT TO IMPROVE?

1.

2.

3.

HOW DO YOU FEEL IN YOUR BODY?

WHO HELD YOU ACCOUNTABLE?

Notes, Quotes, and Relfections

TIME TO ORDER YOUR NEXT PLANNER!

Yay! You showed up strong and consistently!!! Celebrate the heck out of yourself today!

Go order your next copy so you don't skip a beat!! You deserve it!

Need more help? Contact Krystalore for questions or for other private and group coaching programs to help fuel you forward!

I'm in your corner, reach out today!

Month
THREE

Notes, Quotes, and Relfections

Monthly Intentions

THE THIRD MONTH

Month _____ *Date* _____

GOALS FOR THE MONTH

WHO/WHAT AM I GRATEFUL FOR?

THE "I GET TO" LIST

- [ ] _____
- [ ] _____
- [ ] _____
- [ ] _____
- [ ] _____
- [ ] _____
- [ ] _____
- [ ] _____
- [ ] _____
- [ ] _____

HOW WILL I SHOW UP THIS MONTH FOR MY PEOPLE?

Week One

SETTING INTENTIONS

Month _____ *Date* _____

PICK ONE GOAL TO FOCUS ON THIS WEEK:

MON	
TUES	
WED	
THURS	
FRI	
SAT	
SUN	

I "GET TO" LIST

⬡
⬡
⬡
⬡

NOTES

SOCIAL INTENTIONS

1.

2.

3.

Notes, Quotes, and Relfections

MORNING PAGE

Day _____ *Date* _____

DAILY SCHEDULE

6:00

7:00

8:00

9:00

10:00

11:00

12:00

1:00

2:00

3:00

4:00

5:00

6:00

7:00

8:00

I AM GRATEFUL FOR...

I AM STATEMENT ...

#1 GOAL TODAY

TOP 5 PRIORITIES

1.

2.

3.

4.

5.

WHO NEEDS ME AT 100% TODAY?

WHO CAN I MAKE SMILE TODAY?

EVENING PAGE

Day _____ *Date* _____

EVENING REFLECTIONS

MY BIG WINS TODAY

HOW DID I FEEL TODAY?

HOW DID I SHOW UP FOR THE PEOPLE IN MY LIFE TODAY?

HOW INTENTIONAL WAS I?

① ② ③ ④ ⑤

WATER? ☐   WORKOUT? ☐

WHAT GOT IN THE WAY?

1.

2.

3.

WHAT WILL I DO DIFFERENT?

MORNING PAGE

Day _____ *Date* _____

DAILY SCHEDULE	I AM GRATEFUL FOR...
6:00	
7:00	
8:00	
9:00	
10:00	**I AM STATEMENT ...**
11:00	
12:00	**#1 GOAL TODAY**
1:00	
2:00	**TOP 5 PRIORITIES**
3:00	*1.*
	2.
4:00	*3.*
	4.
5:00	*5.*
6:00	**WHO NEEDS ME AT 100% TODAY?**
7:00	**WHO CAN I MAKE SMILE TODAY?**
8:00	

EVENING PAGE

Day _____ Date _____

EVENING REFLECTIONS

MY BIG WINS TODAY

HOW DID I FEEL TODAY?

HOW DID I SHOW UP FOR THE PEOPLE IN MY LIFE TODAY?

HOW INTENTIONAL WAS I?

① ② ③ ④ ⑤

WATER? ☐   WORKOUT? ☐

WHAT GOT IN THE WAY?

1.

2.

3.

WHAT WILL I DO DIFFERENT?

MORNING PAGE

Day —————— *Date* ——————

DAILY SCHEDULE	I AM GRATEFUL FOR...
6:00	
7:00	
8:00	
9:00	
10:00	**I AM STATEMENT ...**
11:00	
12:00	**#1 GOAL TODAY**
1:00	
2:00	**TOP 5 PRIORITIES**
3:00	*1.*
	2.
	3.
4:00	*4.*
5:00	*5.*
6:00	**WHO NEEDS ME AT 100% TODAY?**
7:00	**WHO CAN I MAKE SMILE TODAY?**
8:00	

EVENING PAGE

Day ———————— *Date* ————————

EVENING REFLECTIONS

HOW DID I SHOW UP FOR THE PEOPLE IN MY LIFE TODAY?

MY BIG WINS TODAY

HOW INTENTIONAL WAS I?

① ② ③ ④ ⑤

WATER? ☐   WORKOUT? ☐

WHAT GOT IN THE WAY?

1.

2.

3.

HOW DID I FEEL TODAY?

WHAT WILL I DO DIFFERENT?

MORNING PAGE

Day _____ *Date* _____

DAILY SCHEDULE

6:00
7:00
8:00
9:00
10:00
11:00
12:00
1:00
2:00
3:00
4:00
5:00
6:00
7:00
8:00

I AM GRATEFUL FOR...

I AM STATEMENT ...

#1 GOAL TODAY

TOP 5 PRIORITIES

1.

2.

3.

4.

5.

WHO NEEDS ME AT 100% TODAY?

WHO CAN I MAKE SMILE TODAY?

EVENING PAGE

Day _____ *Date* _____

EVENING REFLECTIONS

MY BIG WINS TODAY

HOW DID I SHOW UP FOR THE PEOPLE IN MY LIFE TODAY?

HOW INTENTIONAL WAS I?

(1) (2) (3) (4) (5)

WATER? ☐   WORKOUT? ☐

WHAT GOT IN THE WAY?

1.

2.

3.

HOW DID I FEEL TODAY?

WHAT WILL I DO DIFFERENT?

MORNING PAGE

Day _____ *Date* _____

DAILY SCHEDULE	I AM GRATEFUL FOR...
6:00	
7:00	
8:00	
9:00	
10:00	**I AM STATEMENT ...**
11:00	
12:00	**#1 GOAL TODAY**
1:00	
2:00	**TOP 5 PRIORITIES**
3:00	*1.*
	2.
4:00	*3.*
	4.
5:00	*5.*
6:00	**WHO NEEDS ME AT 100% TODAY?**
7:00	**WHO CAN I MAKE SMILE TODAY?**
8:00	

EVENING PAGE

Day _____ *Date* _____

EVENING REFLECTIONS

HOW DID I SHOW UP FOR THE PEOPLE IN MY LIFE TODAY?

MY BIG WINS TODAY

HOW INTENTIONAL WAS I?

(1) (2) (3) (4) (5)

WATER? ☐   WORKOUT? ☐

WHAT GOT IN THE WAY?

1.
2.
3.

HOW DID I FEEL TODAY?

WHAT WILL I DO DIFFERENT?

MORNING PAGE

Day _____ *Date* _____

DAILY SCHEDULE	I AM GRATEFUL FOR...
6:00	
7:00	
8:00	
9:00	
10:00	**I AM STATEMENT ...**
11:00	
12:00	**#1 GOAL TODAY**
1:00	
2:00	**TOP 5 PRIORITIES**
3:00	1.
	2.
4:00	3.
	4.
5:00	5.
6:00	**WHO NEEDS ME AT 100% TODAY?**
7:00	
	WHO CAN I MAKE SMILE TODAY?
8:00	

EVENING PAGE

Day _____ *Date* _____

EVENING REFLECTIONS

MY BIG WINS TODAY

HOW DID I SHOW UP FOR THE PEOPLE IN MY LIFE TODAY?

HOW INTENTIONAL WAS I?

(1) (2) (3) (4) (5)

WATER? ☐   WORKOUT? ☐

WHAT GOT IN THE WAY?

1.

2.

3.

HOW DID I FEEL TODAY?

WHAT WILL I DO DIFFERENT?

MORNING PAGE

DAILY SCHEDULE

6:00

7:00

8:00

9:00

10:00

11:00

12:00

1:00

2:00

3:00

4:00

5:00

6:00

7:00

8:00

I AM GRATEFUL FOR...

I AM STATEMENT ...

#1 GOAL TODAY

TOP 5 PRIORITIES

1.

2.

3.

4.

5.

WHO NEEDS ME AT 100% TODAY?

WHO CAN I MAKE SMILE TODAY?

EVENING PAGE

Day _____ *Date* _____

EVENING REFLECTIONS

HOW DID I SHOW UP FOR THE PEOPLE IN MY LIFE TODAY?

MY BIG WINS TODAY

HOW INTENTIONAL WAS I?

① ② ③ ④ ⑤

WATER? ☐   WORKOUT? ☐

WHAT GOT IN THE WAY?

1.

2.

3.

HOW DID I FEEL TODAY?

WHAT WILL I DO DIFFERENT?

Week One

WEEKLY REVIEW

Month _____ *Date* _____

INSTRUCTIONS: On a scale of 1-5 (5 being the best-as in I did it every day, 4-almost every day, 3-half the time, 2-barely did what I needed, 1-fell off the wagon this week) how successful were you at your daily intentions for the following:

WORKOUTS: DID YOU MOVE AT LEAST 30 MIN DAILY?

NUTRITION: DID YOU EAT WELL BALANCED MEALS & TRACK EACH DAY(IF TRACKING)? DID YOU EAT TO FUEL FOR YOUR NEEDS & RESULTS YOU DESIRE?

HYDRATION: DID YOU DRINK ENOUGH WATER?
(½ BODY WEIGHT IN OZ PER DAY)

PRIORITIES & ACCOMPLISHMENT: DID YOU ACCOMPLISH EVERYTHING YOU INTENDED? (NOTE UNFINISHED BUSINESS BELOW)

SLEEP: DID YOU GET TO BED EACH NIGHT AND WAKE UP ON TIME? (WHAT DO YOU NEED TO DO DIFFERENTLY NEXT WEEK?

Week In Reflection

Yay! You showed up this week!! What were your biggest reflections, wins, memories, and challenges? How will you use this to fuel you forward into next week?

Week Two

SETTING INTENTIONS

Month _____ *Date* _____

PICK ONE GOAL TO FOCUS ON THIS WEEK:

MON	**I "GET TO" LIST**
TUES	⬡
WED	⬡
	⬡
	⬡
THURS	**NOTES**
FRI	
SAT	**SOCIAL INTENTIONS**
SUN	1.
	2.
	3.

Notes, Quotes, and Relfections

MORNING PAGE

Month _____ *Date* _____

DAILY SCHEDULE	I AM GRATEFUL FOR...
6:00	
7:00	
8:00	
9:00	
10:00	**I AM STATEMENT ...**
11:00	
12:00	**#1 GOAL TODAY**
1:00	
2:00	**TOP 5 PRIORITIES**
3:00	*1.*
4:00	*2.*
5:00	*3.*
	4.
6:00	*5.*
7:00	**WHO NEEDS ME AT 100% TODAY?**
8:00	**WHO CAN I MAKE SMILE TODAY?**

EVENING PAGE

Day _____ *Date* _____

EVENING REFLECTIONS

MY BIG WINS TODAY

HOW DID I FEEL TODAY?

HOW DID I SHOW UP FOR THE PEOPLE IN MY LIFE TODAY?

HOW INTENTIONAL WAS I?

① ② ③ ④ ⑤

WATER? ☐   **WORKOUT?** ☐

WHAT GOT IN THE WAY?

1.

2.

3.

WHAT WILL I DO DIFFERENT?

MORNING PAGE

Day _____ *Date* _____

DAILY SCHEDULE	I AM GRATEFUL FOR...
6:00	
7:00	
8:00	
9:00	
10:00	**I AM STATEMENT ...**
11:00	
12:00	**#1 GOAL TODAY**
1:00	
2:00	**TOP 5 PRIORITIES**
3:00	*1.*
	2.
4:00	*3.*
	4.
5:00	*5.*
6:00	**WHO NEEDS ME AT 100% TODAY?**
7:00	
	WHO CAN I MAKE SMILE TODAY?
8:00	

EVENING PAGE

Day _____ *Date* _____

EVENING REFLECTIONS

HOW DID I SHOW UP FOR THE PEOPLE IN MY LIFE TODAY?

MY BIG WINS TODAY

HOW INTENTIONAL WAS I?

① ② ③ ④ ⑤

WATER? ☐   WORKOUT? ☐

WHAT GOT IN THE WAY?

1.

2.

3.

HOW DID I FEEL TODAY?

WHAT WILL I DO DIFFERENT?

MORNING PAGE

Day _____ *Date* _____

DAILY SCHEDULE	I AM GRATEFUL FOR...
6:00	
7:00	
8:00	
9:00	
10:00	**I AM STATEMENT ...**
11:00	
12:00	**#1 GOAL TODAY**
1:00	
2:00	**TOP 5 PRIORITIES**
	1.
3:00	*2.*
	3.
4:00	*4.*
5:00	*5.*
6:00	**WHO NEEDS ME AT 100% TODAY?**
7:00	**WHO CAN I MAKE SMILE TODAY?**
8:00	

EVENING PAGE

Day _____ *Date* _____

EVENING REFLECTIONS

MY BIG WINS TODAY

HOW DID I FEEL TODAY?

HOW DID I SHOW UP FOR THE PEOPLE IN MY LIFE TODAY?

HOW INTENTIONAL WAS I?

① ② ③ ④ ⑤

WATER? ☐   WORKOUT? ☐

WHAT GOT IN THE WAY?

1.
2.
3.

WHAT WILL I DO DIFFERENT?

MORNING PAGE

Day _____ *Date* _____

DAILY SCHEDULE	I AM GRATEFUL FOR...
6:00	
7:00	
8:00	
9:00	
10:00	**I AM STATEMENT ...**
11:00	
12:00	**#1 GOAL TODAY**
1:00	
2:00	**TOP 5 PRIORITIES**
3:00	*1.*
	2.
4:00	*3.*
	4.
5:00	*5.*
6:00	**WHO NEEDS ME AT 100% TODAY?**
7:00	**WHO CAN I MAKE SMILE TODAY?**
8:00	

EVENING PAGE

Day _____ *Date* _____

EVENING REFLECTIONS

HOW DID I SHOW UP FOR THE PEOPLE IN MY LIFE TODAY?

MY BIG WINS TODAY

HOW INTENTIONAL WAS I?

(1) (2) (3) (4) (5)

WATER? ☐   WORKOUT? ☐

WHAT GOT IN THE WAY?

1.

2.

3.

HOW DID I FEEL TODAY?

WHAT WILL I DO DIFFERENT?

MORNING PAGE

Day _____ *Date* _____

DAILY SCHEDULE	I AM GRATEFUL FOR...
6:00	
7:00	
8:00	
9:00	
10:00	**I AM STATEMENT ...**
11:00	
12:00	**#1 GOAL TODAY**
1:00	
2:00	**TOP 5 PRIORITIES**
3:00	*1.*
4:00	*2.*
5:00	*3.*
	4.
	5.
6:00	**WHO NEEDS ME AT 100% TODAY?**
7:00	**WHO CAN I MAKE SMILE TODAY?**
8:00	

EVENING PAGE

Day _____ *Date* _____

EVENING REFLECTIONS

HOW DID I SHOW UP FOR THE PEOPLE IN MY LIFE TODAY?

MY BIG WINS TODAY

HOW INTENTIONAL WAS I?

① ② ③ ④ ⑤

WATER? ☐   WORKOUT? ☐

WHAT GOT IN THE WAY?

1.

2.

3.

HOW DID I FEEL TODAY?

WHAT WILL I DO DIFFERENT?

MORNING PAGE

Day _____ *Date* _____

DAILY SCHEDULE	I AM GRATEFUL FOR...
6:00	⬡
7:00	⬡
8:00	⬡
9:00	

I AM STATEMENT ...

#1 GOAL TODAY

6:00

TOP 5 PRIORITIES

Daily schedule continued (left column):

- 6:00
- 7:00
- 8:00
- 9:00
- 10:00
- 11:00
- 12:00
- 1:00
- 2:00
- 3:00
- 4:00
- 5:00
- 6:00
- 7:00
- 8:00

TOP 5 PRIORITIES

1.
2.
3.
4.
5.

WHO NEEDS ME AT 100% TODAY?

WHO CAN I MAKE SMILE TODAY?

EVENING PAGE

Day _____ *Date* _____

EVENING REFLECTIONS

MY BIG WINS TODAY

HOW DID I FEEL TODAY?

HOW DID I SHOW UP FOR THE PEOPLE IN MY LIFE TODAY?

HOW INTENTIONAL WAS I?

① ② ③ ④ ⑤

WATER? ☐   WORKOUT? ☐

WHAT GOT IN THE WAY?

1.
2.
3.

WHAT WILL I DO DIFFERENT?

MORNING PAGE

Day _____ *Date* _____

DAILY SCHEDULE	I AM GRATEFUL FOR...
6:00	
7:00	
8:00	
9:00	
10:00	**I AM STATEMENT ...**
11:00	
12:00	**#1 GOAL TODAY**
1:00	
2:00	**TOP 5 PRIORITIES**
3:00	*1.*
	2.
4:00	*3.*
	4.
5:00	*5.*
6:00	**WHO NEEDS ME AT 100% TODAY?**
7:00	**WHO CAN I MAKE SMILE TODAY?**
8:00	

EVENING PAGE

Day _____ *Date* _____

EVENING REFLECTIONS

HOW DID I SHOW UP FOR THE PEOPLE IN MY LIFE TODAY?

MY BIG WINS TODAY

HOW INTENTIONAL WAS I?

① ② ③ ④ ⑤

WATER? ☐   WORKOUT? ☐

WHAT GOT IN THE WAY?

1.
2.
3.

HOW DID I FEEL TODAY?

WHAT WILL I DO DIFFERENT?

Week Two

INSTRUCTIONS: On a scale of 1-5 (5 being the best-as in I did it every day, 4-almost every day, 3-half the time, 2-barely did what I needed, 1-fell off the wagon this week) how successful were you at your daily intentions for the following:

⬡ **WORKOUTS:** DID YOU MOVE AT LEAST 30 MIN DAILY?

⬡ **NUTRITION:** DID YOU EAT WELL BALANCED MEALS & TRACK EACH DAY(IF TRACKING)? DID YOU EAT TO FUEL FOR YOUR NEEDS & RESULTS YOU DESIRE?

⬡ **HYDRATION:** DID YOU DRINK ENOUGH WATER?
(½ BODY WEIGHT IN OZ PER DAY)

⬡ **PRIORITIES & ACCOMPLISHMENT:** DID YOU ACCOMPLISH EVERYTHING YOU INTENDED? (NOTE UNFINISHED BUSINESS BELOW)

⬡ **SLEEP:** DID YOU GET TO BED EACH NIGHT AND WAKE UP ON TIME? (WHAT DO YOU NEED TO DO DIFFERENTLY NEXT WEEK?

Week In Reflection

Yay! You showed up this week!! What were your biggest reflections, wins, memories, and challenges? How will you use this to fuel you forward into next week?

Week Three

SETTING INTENTIONS

"Crews Beyond Limits is not a fad, it's a lifestyle." -Krystalore Crews

PICK ONE GOAL TO FOCUS ON THIS WEEK:

MON	
TUES	
WED	
THURS	
FRI	
SAT	
SUN	

I "GET TO" LIST

NOTES

SOCIAL INTENTIONS

1.

2.

3.

Notes, Quotes, and Relfections

MORNING PAGE

Day _____ *Date* _____

DAILY SCHEDULE	I AM GRATEFUL FOR...
6:00	
7:00	
8:00	
9:00	
10:00	**I AM STATEMENT ...**
11:00	**#1 GOAL TODAY**
12:00	
1:00	**TOP 5 PRIORITIES**
2:00	*1.*
3:00	*2.*
	3.
4:00	*4.*
5:00	*5.*
6:00	**WHO NEEDS ME AT 100% TODAY?**
7:00	**WHO CAN I MAKE SMILE TODAY?**
8:00	

EVENING PAGE

Day _____ *Date* _____

EVENING REFLECTIONS

MY BIG WINS TODAY

HOW DID I FEEL TODAY?

HOW DID I SHOW UP FOR THE PEOPLE IN MY LIFE TODAY?

HOW INTENTIONAL WAS I?

① ② ③ ④ ⑤

WATER? ☐   WORKOUT? ☐

WHAT GOT IN THE WAY?

1.

2.

3.

WHAT WILL I DO DIFFERENT?

MORNING PAGE

Day _____ *Date* _____

DAILY SCHEDULE	I AM GRATEFUL FOR...
6:00	
7:00	
8:00	
9:00	
10:00	**I AM STATEMENT ...**
11:00	
12:00	**#1 GOAL TODAY**
1:00	
2:00	**TOP 5 PRIORITIES**
3:00	*1.*
	2.
4:00	*3.*
	4.
5:00	*5.*
6:00	**WHO NEEDS ME AT 100% TODAY?**
7:00	**WHO CAN I MAKE SMILE TODAY?**
8:00	

EVENING PAGE

Day _____ *Date* _____

EVENING REFLECTIONS

HOW DID I SHOW UP FOR THE PEOPLE IN MY LIFE TODAY?

MY BIG WINS TODAY

HOW INTENTIONAL WAS I?

① ② ③ ④ ⑤

WATER? ☐   WORKOUT? ☐

WHAT GOT IN THE WAY?

1.
2.
3.

HOW DID I FEEL TODAY?

WHAT WILL I DO DIFFERENT?

MORNING PAGE

Day _____ *Date* _____

DAILY SCHEDULE	I AM GRATEFUL FOR...
6:00	
7:00	
8:00	
9:00	
10:00	**I AM STATEMENT ...**
11:00	
12:00	**#1 GOAL TODAY**
1:00	
2:00	**TOP 5 PRIORITIES**
3:00	*1.*
	2.
4:00	*3.*
	4.
5:00	*5.*
6:00	**WHO NEEDS ME AT 100% TODAY?**
7:00	**WHO CAN I MAKE SMILE TODAY?**
8:00	

EVENING PAGE

Day _____ *Date* _____

EVENING REFLECTIONS

MY BIG WINS TODAY

HOW DID I SHOW UP FOR THE PEOPLE IN MY LIFE TODAY?

HOW INTENTIONAL WAS I?

(1) (2) (3) (4) (5)

WATER? ☐   WORKOUT? ☐

WHAT GOT IN THE WAY?

1.
2.
3.

HOW DID I FEEL TODAY?

WHAT WILL I DO DIFFERENT?

MORNING PAGE

DAILY SCHEDULE	I AM GRATEFUL FOR...
6:00	
7:00	
8:00	
9:00	
10:00	**I AM STATEMENT ...**
11:00	**#1 GOAL TODAY**
12:00	
1:00	**TOP 5 PRIORITIES**
2:00	*1.*
3:00	*2.*
	3.
4:00	*4.*
5:00	*5.*
6:00	**WHO NEEDS ME AT 100% TODAY?**
7:00	**WHO CAN I MAKE SMILE TODAY?**
8:00	

EVENING PAGE

Day _____ *Date* _____

EVENING REFLECTIONS

MY BIG WINS TODAY

HOW DID I FEEL TODAY?

HOW DID I SHOW UP FOR THE PEOPLE IN MY LIFE TODAY?

HOW INTENTIONAL WAS I?

(1) (2) (3) (4) (5)

WATER? ☐   WORKOUT? ☐

WHAT GOT IN THE WAY?

1.

2.

3.

WHAT WILL I DO DIFFERENT?

MORNING PAGE

Day _____ *Date* _____

DAILY SCHEDULE	I AM GRATEFUL FOR...
6:00	
7:00	
8:00	
9:00	

I AM STATEMENT ...

#1 GOAL TODAY

TOP 5 PRIORITIES

1.

2.

3.

4.

5.

WHO NEEDS ME AT 100% TODAY?

WHO CAN I MAKE SMILE TODAY?

Daily Schedule times: 6:00, 7:00, 8:00, 9:00, 10:00, 11:00, 12:00, 1:00, 2:00, 3:00, 4:00, 5:00, 6:00, 7:00, 8:00

EVENING PAGE

Day _____ *Date* _____

EVENING REFLECTIONS

HOW DID I SHOW UP FOR THE PEOPLE IN MY LIFE TODAY?

MY BIG WINS TODAY

HOW INTENTIONAL WAS I?

(1) (2) (3) (4) (5)

WATER? ☐   WORKOUT? ☐

WHAT GOT IN THE WAY?

1.

2.

3.

HOW DID I FEEL TODAY?

WHAT WILL I DO DIFFERENT?

MORNING PAGE

Day _____ *Date* _____

DAILY SCHEDULE	I AM GRATEFUL FOR...
6:00	
7:00	
8:00	
9:00	
10:00	**I AM STATEMENT ...**
11:00	**#1 GOAL TODAY**
12:00	
1:00	
2:00	**TOP 5 PRIORITIES**
3:00	*1.*
	2.
	3.
4:00	*4.*
5:00	*5.*
6:00	**WHO NEEDS ME AT 100% TODAY?**
7:00	**WHO CAN I MAKE SMILE TODAY?**
8:00	

EVENING PAGE

Day _____ *Date* _____

EVENING REFLECTIONS

HOW DID I SHOW UP FOR THE PEOPLE IN MY LIFE TODAY?

MY BIG WINS TODAY

HOW INTENTIONAL WAS I?

① ② ③ ④ ⑤

WATER? ☐   WORKOUT? ☐

WHAT GOT IN THE WAY?

1.

2.

3.

HOW DID I FEEL TODAY?

WHAT WILL I DO DIFFERENT?

MORNING PAGE

Day _____ *Date* _____

DAILY SCHEDULE	I AM GRATEFUL FOR...
6:00	
7:00	
8:00	
9:00	
10:00	**I AM STATEMENT ...**
11:00	
12:00	**#1 GOAL TODAY**
1:00	
2:00	**TOP 5 PRIORITIES**
3:00	*1.*
	2.
4:00	*3.*
	4.
5:00	*5.*
6:00	**WHO NEEDS ME AT 100% TODAY?**
7:00	**WHO CAN I MAKE SMILE TODAY?**
8:00	

EVENING PAGE

Day _____ *Date* _____

EVENING REFLECTIONS

MY BIG WINS TODAY

HOW DID I FEEL TODAY?

HOW DID I SHOW UP FOR THE PEOPLE IN MY LIFE TODAY?

HOW INTENTIONAL WAS I?

① ② ③ ④ ⑤

WATER? ☐   **WORKOUT?** ☐

WHAT GOT IN THE WAY?

1.

2.

3.

WHAT WILL I DO DIFFERENT?

Week Three

WEEKLY REVIEW

INSTRUCTIONS: On a scale of 1-5 (5 being the best-as in I did it every day, 4-almost every day, 3-half the time, 2-barely did what I needed, 1-fell off the wagon this week) how successful were you at your daily intentions for the following:

WORKOUTS: DID YOU MOVE AT LEAST 30 MIN DAILY?

NUTRITION: DID YOU EAT WELL BALANCED MEALS & TRACK EACH DAY(IF TRACKING)? DID YOU EAT TO FUEL FOR YOUR NEEDS & RESULTS YOU DESIRE?

HYDRATION: DID YOU DRINK ENOUGH WATER?
(½ BODY WEIGHT IN OZ PER DAY)

PRIORITIES & ACCOMPLISHMENT: DID YOU ACCOMPLISH EVERYTHING YOU INTENDED? (NOTE UNFINISHED BUSINESS BELOW)

SLEEP: DID YOU GET TO BED EACH NIGHT AND WAKE UP ON TIME? (WHAT DO YOU NEED TO DO DIFFERENTLY NEXT WEEK?

Week In Reflection

Yay! You showed up this week!! What were your biggest reflections, wins, memories, and challenges? How will you use this to fuel you forward into next week?

Week Four

SETTING INTENTIONS

"We don't just 'arrive' at Bombshell status. Small movements lead to huge results. We must honor the journey, set intentions, and celebrate every step of the way."
-Krystalore Crews

PICK ONE GOAL TO FOCUS ON THIS WEEK:

MON	
TUES	
WED	
THURS	
FRI	
SAT	
SUN	

I "GET TO" LIST

NOTES

SOCIAL INTENTIONS

1.

2.

3.

Notes, Quotes, and Relfections

MORNING PAGE

Day _____ *Date* _____

DAILY SCHEDULE	I AM GRATEFUL FOR...
6:00	
7:00	
8:00	
9:00	
10:00	**I AM STATEMENT ...**
11:00	
12:00	**#1 GOAL TODAY**
1:00	
2:00	**TOP 5 PRIORITIES**
3:00	*1.*
	2.
4:00	*3.*
	4.
5:00	*5.*
6:00	**WHO NEEDS ME AT 100% TODAY?**
7:00	
	WHO CAN I MAKE SMILE TODAY?
8:00	

EVENING PAGE

Day _____ *Date* _____

EVENING REFLECTIONS

HOW DID I SHOW UP FOR THE PEOPLE IN MY LIFE TODAY?

MY BIG WINS TODAY

HOW INTENTIONAL WAS I?

① ② ③ ④ ⑤

WATER? ☐   WORKOUT? ☐

WHAT GOT IN THE WAY?

1.
2.
3.

HOW DID I FEEL TODAY?

WHAT WILL I DO DIFFERENT?

MORNING PAGE

Day _____ *Date* _____

DAILY SCHEDULE	I AM GRATEFUL FOR...
6:00	
7:00	
8:00	
9:00	
10:00	**I AM STATEMENT ...**
11:00	
	#1 GOAL TODAY
12:00	
1:00	**TOP 5 PRIORITIES**
2:00	1.
3:00	2.
	3.
4:00	4.
5:00	5.
6:00	**WHO NEEDS ME AT 100% TODAY?**
7:00	**WHO CAN I MAKE SMILE TODAY?**
8:00	

EVENING PAGE

Day _____ *Date* _____

EVENING REFLECTIONS

HOW DID I SHOW UP FOR THE PEOPLE IN MY LIFE TODAY?

MY BIG WINS TODAY

HOW INTENTIONAL WAS I?

① ② ③ ④ ⑤

WATER? ☐   WORKOUT? ☐

WHAT GOT IN THE WAY?

1.
2.
3.

HOW DID I FEEL TODAY?

WHAT WILL I DO DIFFERENT?

MORNING PAGE

Day _____ *Date* _____

DAILY SCHEDULE	I AM GRATEFUL FOR...
6:00	
7:00	
8:00	
9:00	
10:00	**I AM STATEMENT ...**
11:00	
12:00	**#1 GOAL TODAY**
1:00	
2:00	**TOP 5 PRIORITIES**
3:00	1.
	2.
4:00	3.
	4.
5:00	5.
6:00	**WHO NEEDS ME AT 100% TODAY?**
7:00	**WHO CAN I MAKE SMILE TODAY?**
8:00	

EVENING PAGE

Day _____ *Date* _____

EVENING REFLECTIONS

HOW DID I SHOW UP FOR THE PEOPLE IN MY LIFE TODAY?

MY BIG WINS TODAY

HOW INTENTIONAL WAS I?

① ② ③ ④ ⑤

WATER? ☐   WORKOUT? ☐

WHAT GOT IN THE WAY?

1.
2.
3.

HOW DID I FEEL TODAY?

WHAT WILL I DO DIFFERENT?

MORNING PAGE

Day _____ *Date* _____

DAILY SCHEDULE	I AM GRATEFUL FOR...
6:00	
7:00	
8:00	
9:00	
10:00	**I AM STATEMENT ...**
11:00	
12:00	**#1 GOAL TODAY**
1:00	
2:00	**TOP 5 PRIORITIES**
3:00	*1.*
	2.
4:00	*3.*
	4.
5:00	*5.*
6:00	**WHO NEEDS ME AT 100% TODAY?**
7:00	**WHO CAN I MAKE SMILE TODAY?**
8:00	

EVENING PAGE

Day _____ *Date* _____

EVENING REFLECTIONS

HOW DID I SHOW UP FOR THE PEOPLE IN MY LIFE TODAY?

MY BIG WINS TODAY

HOW INTENTIONAL WAS I?

① ② ③ ④ ⑤

WATER? ☐   WORKOUT? ☐

WHAT GOT IN THE WAY?

1. _____
2. _____
3. _____

HOW DID I FEEL TODAY?

WHAT WILL I DO DIFFERENT?

MORNING PAGE

Day _____ *Date* _____

DAILY SCHEDULE	I AM GRATEFUL FOR...
6:00	
7:00	
8:00	
9:00	
10:00	**I AM STATEMENT ...**
11:00	
12:00	**#1 GOAL TODAY**
1:00	**TOP 5 PRIORITIES**
2:00	*1.*
3:00	*2.*
	3.
4:00	*4.*
5:00	*5.*
6:00	**WHO NEEDS ME AT 100% TODAY?**
7:00	
	WHO CAN I MAKE SMILE TODAY?
8:00	

EVENING PAGE

Day _____ *Date* _____

EVENING REFLECTIONS

HOW DID I SHOW UP FOR THE PEOPLE IN MY LIFE TODAY?

MY BIG WINS TODAY

HOW INTENTIONAL WAS I?

(1) (2) (3) (4) (5)

WATER? ☐   WORKOUT? ☐

WHAT GOT IN THE WAY?

1.

2.

3.

HOW DID I FEEL TODAY?

WHAT WILL I DO DIFFERENT?

MORNING PAGE

Day _____ *Date* _____

DAILY SCHEDULE	I AM GRATEFUL FOR...
6:00	
7:00	
8:00	
9:00	
10:00	**I AM STATEMENT ...**
11:00	
12:00	**#1 GOAL TODAY**
1:00	
2:00	**TOP 5 PRIORITIES**
3:00	1.
	2.
4:00	3.
	4.
5:00	5.
6:00	**WHO NEEDS ME AT 100% TODAY?**
7:00	**WHO CAN I MAKE SMILE TODAY?**
8:00	

EVENING PAGE

Day _____ *Date* _____

EVENING REFLECTIONS

MY BIG WINS TODAY

HOW DID I SHOW UP FOR THE PEOPLE IN MY LIFE TODAY?

HOW INTENTIONAL WAS I?

(1) (2) (3) (4) (5)

WATER? ☐   WORKOUT? ☐

WHAT GOT IN THE WAY?

1.
2.
3.

HOW DID I FEEL TODAY?

WHAT WILL I DO DIFFERENT?

MORNING PAGE

Day _____ *Date* _____

DAILY SCHEDULE

6:00

7:00

8:00

9:00

10:00

11:00

12:00

1:00

2:00

3:00

4:00

5:00

6:00

7:00

8:00

I AM GRATEFUL FOR...

I AM STATEMENT ...

#1 GOAL TODAY

TOP 5 PRIORITIES

1.

2.

3.

4.

5.

WHO NEEDS ME AT 100% TODAY?

WHO CAN I MAKE SMILE TODAY?

EVENING PAGE

Day _____ *Date* _____

EVENING REFLECTIONS

MY BIG WINS TODAY

HOW DID I FEEL TODAY?

HOW DID I SHOW UP FOR THE PEOPLE IN MY LIFE TODAY?

HOW INTENTIONAL WAS I?

① ② ③ ④ ⑤

WATER? ☐   WORKOUT? ☐

WHAT GOT IN THE WAY?

1.

2.

3.

WHAT WILL I DO DIFFERENT?

Week Four

WEEKLY REVIEW

Month ——————— *Date* ———————

INSTRUCTIONS: On a scale of 1-5 (5 being the best-as in I did it every day, 4-almost every day, 3-half the time, 2-barely did what I needed, 1-fell off the wagon this week) how successful were you at your daily intentions for the following:

⬡ **WORKOUTS:** DID YOU MOVE AT LEAST 30 MIN DAILY?

⬡ **NUTRITION:** DID YOU EAT WELL BALANCED MEALS & TRACK EACH DAY(IF TRACKING)? DID YOU EAT TO FUEL FOR YOUR NEEDS & RESULTS YOU DESIRE?

⬡ **HYDRATION:** DID YOU DRINK ENOUGH WATER?
(½ BODY WEIGHT IN OZ PER DAY)

⬡ **PRIORITIES & ACCOMPLISHMENT:** DID YOU ACCOMPLISH EVERYTHING YOU INTENDED? (NOTE UNFINISHED BUSINESS BELOW)

⬡ **SLEEP:** DID YOU GET TO BED EACH NIGHT AND WAKE UP ON TIME? (WHAT DO YOU NEED TO DO DIFFERENTLY NEXT WEEK?

Week In Reflection

Yay! You showed up this week!! What were your biggest reflections, wins, memories, and challenges? How will you use this to fuel you forward into next week?

Week Five

SETTING INTENTIONS

Month _____ *Date* _____

PICK ONE GOAL TO FOCUS ON THIS WEEK:

MON	**I "GET TO" LIST**
TUES	⬡
	⬡
WED	⬡
	⬡
	NOTES
THURS	
FRI	
SAT	**SOCIAL INTENTIONS**
	1.
SUN	2.
	3.

Notes, Quotes, and Relfections

MORNING PAGE

Day _____ *Date* _____

DAILY SCHEDULE	I AM GRATEFUL FOR...
6:00	
7:00	
8:00	
9:00	
10:00	**I AM STATEMENT ...**
11:00	
12:00	**#1 GOAL TODAY**
1:00	
2:00	**TOP 5 PRIORITIES**
3:00	*1.*
	2.
4:00	*3.*
	4.
5:00	*5.*
6:00	**WHO NEEDS ME AT 100% TODAY?**
7:00	**WHO CAN I MAKE SMILE TODAY?**
8:00	

EVENING PAGE

Day _____ *Date* _____

EVENING REFLECTIONS

HOW DID I SHOW UP FOR THE PEOPLE IN MY LIFE TODAY?

MY BIG WINS TODAY

HOW INTENTIONAL WAS I?

① ② ③ ④ ⑤

WATER? ☐   WORKOUT? ☐

WHAT GOT IN THE WAY?

1.
2.
3.

HOW DID I FEEL TODAY?

WHAT WILL I DO DIFFERENT?

MORNING PAGE

Day _____ *Date* _____

DAILY SCHEDULE

6:00

7:00

8:00

9:00

10:00

11:00

12:00

1:00

2:00

3:00

4:00

5:00

6:00

7:00

8:00

I AM GRATEFUL FOR...

I AM STATEMENT ...

#1 GOAL TODAY

TOP 5 PRIORITIES

1.

2.

3.

4.

5.

WHO NEEDS ME AT 100% TODAY?

WHO CAN I MAKE SMILE TODAY?

EVENING PAGE

Day _____ *Date* _____

EVENING REFLECTIONS

HOW DID I SHOW UP FOR THE PEOPLE IN MY LIFE TODAY?

MY BIG WINS TODAY

HOW INTENTIONAL WAS I?

1   2   3   4   5

WATER? ☐   WORKOUT? ☐

WHAT GOT IN THE WAY?

1.

2.

3.

HOW DID I FEEL TODAY?

WHAT WILL I DO DIFFERENT?

MORNING PAGE

Day _____ *Date* _____

DAILY SCHEDULE	I AM GRATEFUL FOR...
6:00	
7:00	
8:00	
9:00	
10:00	**I AM STATEMENT ...**
11:00	
12:00	**#1 GOAL TODAY**
1:00	
2:00	**TOP 5 PRIORITIES**
3:00	*1.*
	2.
4:00	*3.*
	4.
5:00	*5.*
6:00	**WHO NEEDS ME AT 100% TODAY?**
7:00	**WHO CAN I MAKE SMILE TODAY?**
8:00	

EVENING PAGE

Day _____ *Date* _____

EVENING REFLECTIONS

HOW DID I SHOW UP FOR THE PEOPLE IN MY LIFE TODAY?

MY BIG WINS TODAY

HOW INTENTIONAL WAS I?

(1) (2) (3) (4) (5)

WATER? ☐   WORKOUT? ☐

WHAT GOT IN THE WAY?

1.
2.
3.

HOW DID I FEEL TODAY?

WHAT WILL I DO DIFFERENT?

MORNING PAGE

Day _____ *Date* _____

DAILY SCHEDULE	I AM GRATEFUL FOR...
6:00	
7:00	
8:00	
9:00	
10:00	**I AM STATEMENT ...**
11:00	
12:00	**#1 GOAL TODAY**
1:00	
2:00	**TOP 5 PRIORITIES**
3:00	*1.*
	2.
4:00	*3.*
	4.
5:00	*5.*
6:00	**WHO NEEDS ME AT 100% TODAY?**
7:00	**WHO CAN I MAKE SMILE TODAY?**
8:00	

EVENING PAGE

Day _____ *Date* _____

EVENING REFLECTIONS

HOW DID I SHOW UP FOR THE PEOPLE IN MY LIFE TODAY?

MY BIG WINS TODAY

HOW INTENTIONAL WAS I?

(1) (2) (3) (4) (5)

WATER? ☐   WORKOUT? ☐

WHAT GOT IN THE WAY?

1.

2.

3.

HOW DID I FEEL TODAY?

WHAT WILL I DO DIFFERENT?

MORNING PAGE

Day _____ *Date* _____

DAILY SCHEDULE	I AM GRATEFUL FOR...

DAILY SCHEDULE

6:00

7:00

8:00

9:00

10:00

11:00

12:00

1:00

2:00

3:00

4:00

5:00

6:00

7:00

8:00

I AM GRATEFUL FOR...

I AM STATEMENT ...

#1 GOAL TODAY

TOP 5 PRIORITIES

1.

2.

3.

4.

5.

WHO NEEDS ME AT 100% TODAY?

WHO CAN I MAKE SMILE TODAY?

EVENING PAGE

Day _____ *Date* _____

EVENING REFLECTIONS

HOW DID I SHOW UP FOR THE PEOPLE IN MY LIFE TODAY?

MY BIG WINS TODAY

HOW INTENTIONAL WAS I?

① ② ③ ④ ⑤

WATER? ☐   WORKOUT? ☐

WHAT GOT IN THE WAY?

1.

2.

3.

HOW DID I FEEL TODAY?

WHAT WILL I DO DIFFERENT?

MORNING PAGE

Day _____ *Date* _____

DAILY SCHEDULE

6:00

7:00

8:00

9:00

10:00

11:00

12:00

1:00

2:00

3:00

4:00

5:00

6:00

7:00

8:00

I AM GRATEFUL FOR...

I AM STATEMENT ...

#1 GOAL TODAY

TOP 5 PRIORITIES

1.

2.

3.

4.

5.

WHO NEEDS ME AT 100% TODAY?

WHO CAN I MAKE SMILE TODAY?

EVENING PAGE

Day _____ *Date* _____

EVENING REFLECTIONS

MY BIG WINS TODAY

HOW DID I SHOW UP FOR THE PEOPLE IN MY LIFE TODAY?

HOW INTENTIONAL WAS I?

① ② ③ ④ ⑤

WATER? ☐   WORKOUT? ☐

WHAT GOT IN THE WAY?

1.

2.

3.

HOW DID I FEEL TODAY?

WHAT WILL I DO DIFFERENT?

MORNING PAGE

Day _____ *Date* _____

DAILY SCHEDULE	I AM GRATEFUL FOR...
6:00	
7:00	
8:00	
9:00	
10:00	**I AM STATEMENT ...**
11:00	
12:00	**#1 GOAL TODAY**
1:00	
2:00	**TOP 5 PRIORITIES**
3:00	*1.*
	2.
	3.
4:00	*4.*
5:00	*5.*
6:00	**WHO NEEDS ME AT 100% TODAY?**
7:00	**WHO CAN I MAKE SMILE TODAY?**
8:00	

EVENING PAGE

Day _____ *Date* _____

EVENING REFLECTIONS

HOW DID I SHOW UP FOR THE PEOPLE IN MY LIFE TODAY?

MY BIG WINS TODAY

HOW INTENTIONAL WAS I?

① ② ③ ④ ⑤

WATER? ☐   WORKOUT? ☐

WHAT GOT IN THE WAY?

1.

2.

3.

HOW DID I FEEL TODAY?

WHAT WILL I DO DIFFERENT?

Week Five

INSTRUCTIONS: On a scale of 1-5 (5 being the best-as in I did it every day, 4-almost every day, 3-half the time, 2-barely did what I needed, 1-fell off the wagon this week) how successful were you at your daily intentions for the following:

⬡ **WORKOUTS:** DID YOU MOVE AT LEAST 30 MIN DAILY?

⬡ **NUTRITION:** DID YOU EAT WELL BALANCED MEALS & TRACK EACH DAY(IF TRACKING)? DID YOU EAT TO FUEL FOR YOUR NEEDS & RESULTS YOU DESIRE?

⬡ **HYDRATION:** DID YOU DRINK ENOUGH WATER?
(½ BODY WEIGHT IN OZ PER DAY)

⬡ **PRIORITIES & ACCOMPLISHMENT:** DID YOU ACCOMPLISH EVERYTHING YOU INTENDED? (NOTE UNFINISHED BUSINESS BELOW)

⬡ **SLEEP:** DID YOU GET TO BED EACH NIGHT AND WAKE UP ON TIME? (WHAT DO YOU NEED TO DO DIFFERENTLY NEXT WEEK?

Week In Reflection

Yay! You showed up this week!! What were your biggest reflections, wins, memories, and challenges? How will you use this to fuel you forward into next week?

Monthly Review

THE THIRD MONTH

Month _____   *Date* _____

Instructions: Rate your life across all 8 pillars from 1-5.

⬡ Health & Fitness   ⬡ Career   ⬡ Personal Growth   ⬡ Spirituality

⬡ Relationships   ⬡ Social & Liesure ⬡ Quality of Life   ⬡ Finances

CELEBRATING WINS

Share your favorite memories this month:

What are your big wins for this month?

How did you celebrate them?

OVERCOMING OBSTACLES

What "life situation" came up this month that may have derailed you?

How will you overcome it or manage the obstacle?

What would your future self tell you to do today to start momentum?

WHAT DO YOU WANT TO IMPROVE?

1.

2.

3.

HOW DO YOU FEEL IN YOUR BODY?

WHO HELD YOU ACCOUNTABLE?

90 Days In Reflection

Yay! You showed up this last 90 days!! What were your biggest reflections, wins, memories, and challenges? How will you use this to fuel you forward into your next 90 days and beyond?

TIME TO ORDER YOUR NEXT PLANNER!

Yay! You showed up strong and consistently!!! Celebrate the heck out of yourself today!

Go order your next copy so you don't skip a beat!! You deserve it!

Need more help? Contact Krystalore for questions or for other private and group coaching programs to help fuel you forward!

I'm in your corner, reach out today!

Notes, Quotes, and Relfections

What were your biggest reflections, wins, memories, and challenges? How will you use this to fuel you forward into your next 90 days and beyond?

Notes, Quotes, and Relfections

What were your biggest reflections, wins, memories, and challenges? How will you use this to fuel you forward into your next 90 days and beyond?

Notes, Quotes, and Relfections

What were your biggest reflections, wins, memories, and challenges? How will you use this to fuel you forward into your next 90 days and beyond?

CPSIA information can be obtained
at www.ICGtesting.com
Printed in the USA
LVHW061557071121
702655LV00004B/386

9 781737 595403